D1543297

WEAR-EVER'S
Wonderful World of
New Method
Cooking

by Margaret Mitchell

WEAR-EVER'S WONDERFUL WORLD OF NEW METHOD COOKING
by Margaret Mitchell
Third Edition   Copyright   1967
Wear-Ever Aluminum Inc.   Chillicothe, Ohio
Price $2.00

CONGRATULATIONS!

You have opened the door to an exciting new world of food preparation . . . the original Wear-Ever New Method of Cooking.

How proud you'll be of your New Method roasts, pan-broiled meats and poultry which always turn out tender, juicy and digestible when prepared top-stove without added fat or water.

How reassuring to serve your family New Method vegetables and fruits that are rich in minerals and vitamins . . . that retain their garden-fresh colors and natural flavors when cooked over low heat without added water.

You'll marvel at how quick and easy it is to cook New Method meals. There's less peeling and coring, no stirring, pot-watching or boiling over. Your kitchen stays cool and free of cooking odors. And, Wear-Ever's new Stainless Inner-Clad cleans in a jiffy.

If you are economy minded—and who isn't—you'll be happy to discover how soon your Wear-Ever pays for itself through daily New Method savings.

All these exclusive New Method benefits are yours because you have invested in Wear-Ever Stainless Inner-Clad . . . the most beautiful, convenient-to-use and efficient cooking utensils ever made.

When you use Wear-Ever New Method utensils and follow our directions and recipes exactly, every meal will be nutritious and delicious—a real adventure in good eating.

Sincerely,

Margaret Mitchell

Margaret Mitchell
Director of Home Economics
Wear-Ever Aluminum, Inc.

HOW TO COOK THE NEW METHOD WAY

It is easy for even the most inexperienced cook to successfully prepare food by the Wear-Ever New Method of Cooking. There are only three simple rules to follow.

Know the pan to use: At the beginning of each food section we have illustrated the proper pans or combinations to use. For added convenience in selecting the pan specified in a recipe, each utensil has its number stamped on the bottom.

When cooking vegetables and fruits, use the pan the food will most nearly fill along with the cover for that particular pan. Never attempt to cook a small quantity in a large pan.

Know the heat to use: Always use the heat specified in the directions or recipes. New Method cooking is done entirely on Medium-High to Low or Simmer heat. High heat is never used except to bring water to a boil for a beverage or for cooking dried foods. Complete illustrated directions for our heat terms for gas and electric ranges are given on the following page.

If you have a gas range with a Controlled Heat unit known as the "Burner With A Brain", by all means use it for New Method Cooking following directions on pages 6 and 7.

In general: When cooking fruits and vegetables—start on medium heat until first wisps of steam escape or cover is hot to touch—about 5 minutes. Reduce heat to low for remainder of cooking time.

When cooking meats; preheat broiler or roaster pan on medium high heat until a piece of white paper starts to turn brown; reduce heat to medium. Use medium heat to brown all meats. For longer cooking reduce heat to low.

When cooking dried foods; bring water in bottom pan to boil on high heat; reduce heat to low.

When baking on top of the range over direct heat; start on medium heat; reduce heat to low after 5 minutes unless recipe specifies otherwise.

Follow directions and recipes exactly: At first it may be difficult to believe that cooking can be done with such a small amount of heat. The outside of each pan is thick sheet aluminum which conducts heat quickly and evenly. Because of this, foods actually cook from the bottom up, the sides in and the top down. Resist the temptation to turn the heat a little higher. Thousands of tests have proved the heat specified is just right. When cooking fresh vegetables or fruits, never lift the cover until near the end of the cooking time. Frequent removal of cover allows precious moisture to escape and could cause food to burn.

Perfect results with the New Method of Cooking Equipment are yours when you— Select the Right Pan—Use the Proper Heat—Follow Directions Exactly.

IF YOU HAVE AN
ELECTRIC RANGE

USE MEDIUM-HIGH HEAT
Medium-High Switch Position

To preheat utensils for browning meats.
To preheat pan for baking griddle cakes.
Place pan on cold unit, heating gradually
with unit. Do not place cold pan on a hot unit.

USE MEDIUM HEAT
Medium or Medium-Low Switch Position

To brown roast before cooking.
To pan broil steaks, chops, ham slices and hamburgers.
To bake griddle cakes perfectly.
To start fresh fruits, vegetables until
first wisps of steam escape or cover
becomes hot to touch.
To start direct top of range baking.

USE LOW HEAT
Low Switch Position

To cook less tender cuts of meat after browning on all sides.
To cook roasts after browning.
To cook fresh fruits, vegetables after
cover becomes hot to touch.
To steam dried foods over water after water boils.
To do direct top of range baking after
first 5 minutes of baking time.

USE SIMMER HEAT
Simmer Switch Position

To cook fruits, vegetables in No. 780½,
781 and 781½ pans after cover becomes
hot to touch.

IF YOU HAVE A GAS RANGE

USE MEDIUM-HIGH HEAT—flame not quite touching bottom of utensil

To preheat utensils for browning meats.
To preheat pan for baking griddle cakes and French toast.
To boil water over which to steam dried fruits and vegetables.

USE MEDIUM HEAT—flame half as high as medium-high

To brown roasts before cooking.
To pan broil steaks, chops, ham steaks, and hamburgers.
To bake griddle cakes and French toast.
To start fresh fruits, vegetables until first wisps of steam escape or cover becomes hot to touch.
To start direct top of range baking.

USE LOW OR SIMMER HEAT—flame barely visible

To cook less tender cuts of meat after browning on all sides.
To cook roasts after browning.
To cook fresh fruits, vegetables after cover becomes hot to touch.
To steam dried foods over water after water boils.
To do direct top of range baking after first 5 minutes of baking time.

If you have a Gas range equipped with
a "Burner with a Brain"

Place the utensil on the thermostatic or controlled heat top burner so that the sensing element (the "eye" in the center of the burner) comes in contact with the bottom of the utensil. Turn the control to the desired temperature. The sensing element measures the heat in the utensil and will automatically adjust the flame to maintain the set temperature.

The thermostatic top burner may also be equipped with an additional automatic control called "Flame Set" or "Flame Selector." Because Wear-Ever New Method Utensils conduct the heat so evenly, this special control for adjusting the size of the flame is unnecessary and should be disregarded. Follow the simple instructions:

1. Turn dial to "HI" to light burner.
2. Then turn dial to proper temperature for cooking.

When using the "Burner with a Brain" follow the recipes in the book for pre-preparation instruction and the following charts for temperature and time.

FRESH VEGETABLES	DIAL SETTING	TIME (MINUTES)
Asparagus	200°	25–30
Artichokes	200°	40–45
Beans, Green or Yellow	200°	25–30
Beans, Lima	200°	25–30
Beets, sliced	200°	25–30
whole	200°	35–40
Harvard Sauce	200°	5
Beet Greens	190°	18–20
Broccoli	200°	20–25
Brussels Sprouts	200°	25–30
Cabbage, wedges	200°	20
shredded	200°	15
Carrots, sliced or small whole	200°	30–35
Cauliflower, flowerets	200°	15–20
whole	200°	30–35
Celery, diced	200°	25–30
Corn on the Cob	225°	30–35
Eggplant	375°	8–10
Kale	190°	30–35
Kohlrabi, sliced	200°	25
quartered	200°	35
Creamed Mushrooms	200°	8–10
Mushrooms, (pan ⅔ full)		
sliced	175°	30
whole	175°	35
Onions	200°	30–35
Parsnips	200°	35–40
Peas (pan ⅔ full)	200°	20–25
Baked Potatoes	375°	60
Candied Sweet Potatoes	200°	60
to thicken syrup	225°	10
Pumpkin	200°	40–45
Rutabaga, pared, diced	200°	35–40
Spinach	200°	10–12
and Bacon (fry bacon)	275°	5–10
Squash, Summer	200°	15–20
Squash, Winter	200°	30–35

Swiss Chard	200°	12–15
Tomatoes	200°	15–20
Stuffed Tomatoes	200°	20
Turnips	200°	40–45
Hot Potato Salad		
Potatoes	375°	60
Bacon	275°	5–8
Reheat	200°	10–15

FROZEN VEGETABLES

Large size vegetables such as: asparagus, broccoli, Brussels sprouts, cauliflower, spinach	200°	15 minutes; stir; 5–10 minutes longer
Small size vegetables such as: corn, peas, mixed vegetables	200°	10 minutes; stir; 10 minutes; stir; 12–15

FRUITS

Apple Sauce	200°	30–35
Baked Apples	200°	55–60
Grilled Apple Rings	250°	10–15
Glazed Bananas	250°	10–15
Cranberry Jelly	200°	40
Cranberry Sauce	200°	20–25
Spiced Peaches	200°	25
Rhubarb Sauce	200°	10–15
Fruit Curry	200°	15–20

MEATS, FOWL, FISH, EGGS, CHEESE

Roasts—brown at	325°	See recipe
reduce to	225°	See recipe
Meat Loaves	200°	See recipe
Pan Broiling	325°	See recipe
Bacon, frying	275°	5–8 min.
Braising—brown at	325°	See recipe
reduce to	225°	See recipe
Poaching Fish	200°	See recipe
Steaming Fish	212°	See recipe
Eggs	200°	See recipe

DRIED FOODS

Vegetables	212°	1–2 hours
Fruits	212°	30–45

TOP OF RANGE BAKING
CAKE

Coconut Silver Cake	275°	40–45
Butter Cream Cake	275°	35–40
Pineapple Upside Down Cake	275°	45
Prize Spice Cake	275°	45
Cream Sponge Cake	300°	35–40
Angel Food Cake	300°	45

ICINGS

Fluffy Frosting	300°	12

QUICK BREADS

Cornbread	200°	30

SAUCES

Vegetable	200°	8–10
Meat, Fowl, Fish	200°	8–10
Dessert	200°	10–20

GET TO KNOW YOUR
WEAR-EVER BETTER

This trademark identifies genuine Wear-Ever Stainless Inner-Clad Utensils.

THE FIRST cooking utensils ever made of stainless clad aluminum —the modern miracle metal.

THE ONLY cooking utensil approved for New Method of Cooking by the famous Wear-Ever Kitchens.

WEAR-EVER STAINLESS INNER-CLAD

is a thin layer of stainless steel permanently bonded to thick sheet aluminum.

Aluminum outside—spreads heat fast for best cooking results.

Stainless steel inside . . . easy-to-clean, stays lustrous, won't wear off, won't peel off, won't flake off.

HERE'S WHY THICK SHEET ALUMINUM IS SO IMPORTANT

ALUMINUM (SHEET)   .46
AS USED IN WEAR-EVER STAINLESS INNER-CLAD UTENSILS

ALUMINUM (CAST)

ALUMINUM SPREADS HEAT 3 TO 8 TIMES FASTER

STAINLESS STEEL (COPPER CLAD)   .15

STAINLESS STEEL (TRI-PLY)

CAST IRON (PLAIN)   .11

CAST IRON (PORCELAINIZED)

STAINLESS STEEL (PLAIN)   .06

GLASS [CERAMICS]

COMPARATIVE HEAT CONDUCTIVITY

Figures represent C. G. S. units, the scientific scale by which heat conductivity of metals and alloys is measured and compared.

SUPERIOR HEAT CONDUCTIVITY OF THICK SHEET ALUMINUM MAKES POSSIBLE THE WEAR-EVER NEW METHOD OF COOKING.

No additional water is needed with New Method Utensils. The entire pan cooks the food . . . from the bottom up, from the sides in, and from the top down. This avoids hot-spot scorching . . . making it possible for foods to cook in their own natural juices.

Fabulous

Vegetables

VEGETABLES cooked the Wear-Ever New Method way without added water — are Good — a New Taste Treat — Excitingly Different. This is because a maximum of natural flavors, precious vitamins and minerals are kept in the vegetables where they belong. Vegetables, like fruits, are often called the Glow Foods. They help put the sparkle in your eyes, give radiance to your skin and make you feel like a million!

HOW TO PREPARE AND COOK FRESH VEGETABLES

Clean all vegetables well. Slice, dice or leave whole. Place in pan. To save valuable minerals stored next to the skin, do not peel.

Use the sauce pan the vegetable will most nearly fill. The fuller the pan, the less air space which can destroy some vitamins.

Rinse vegetables in pan with cold water. Drain thoroughly, as water like air can destroy some vitamins and minerals. Place cover on pan.

Start cooking on <u>medium</u> heat until first wisps of steam begin to escape or cover is hot to touch —about 5 minutes.

Reduce heat to <u>low</u> for the remainder of cooking time. Test for doneness near end of cooking time as given in cooking chart.

<u>Don't peek!</u> Lifting cover during cooking time lets precious moisture escape. Vegetables should be crisply tender—never overcooked.

WEAR-EVER NEW METHOD UTENSILS FOR VEGETABLES AND FRUITS

782 Sauce Pan and Cover

For larger quantities of diced or sliced vegetables, small whole or bulky vegetables or 2 packages frozen vegetables.

781 ½ Sauce Pan and Cover

For large quantities of diced or sliced vegetables, bulky vegetables or whole vegetable.

For small quantities of diced or sliced vegetables, small whole vegetables or one whole package of frozen vegetables.

780 ½ – 781 Sauce Pan and Cover

480 Food Press

For preparing mashed or riced potatoes, turnips and rutabagas. Pureeing fruits and vegetables.

The mixing bowl is designed especially to fit underneath the food press. Warm the bowl before using for riced hot vegetables.

452 ½ Mixing Bowl

Perfect for cooking just a few ears of corn, fresh green asparagus, broccoli stalks or for baking several apples.

960 Broiler Pan and Cover

VEGETABLE SECRETS: Use only the very freshest vegetables you can find. Prepare according to directions as given in Chart for vegetables, pages 16 and 17. When peeling is absolutely necessary, remove only the thinnest possible layer. All vegetables, except potatoes, are started on <u>medium</u> heat. Because of the cellular structure of potatoes, a slightly higher temperature and preheating of pan is necessary. Medium to small potatoes are cooked whole. Large ones may be halved or quartered, then placed skin side next to pan, cut side toward center.

Since natural minerals are retained, less seasoning is necessary. The amount used should be determined by your own personal taste.

Because vegetables vary in freshness, cooking times listed in the chart are approximate. When a variance in time is given such as 18-20 minutes, test for doneness at the shorter number of minutes, then cook longer if necessary.

Use the Food Press for making mashed or riced potatoes, turnips or squash. The Food Press is also a valuable aid in preparing puréed vegetables for invalids or babies.

To cook fresh or frozen vegetables on a Controlled Heat unit, see chart, pages 6 and 7.

For picture-pretty and delicious-tasting vegetables, prepare properly, select the right pan, rinse, drain, cover, start on <u>medium</u> heat and finish on <u>low</u>. It's as simple as that.

HOW TO COOK FROZEN VEGETABLES

Do not thaw. If vegetable has been frozen into solid block, separate into pieces. Place in sauce pan in frozen state.

Cover; place over <u>medium</u> heat until first wisps of steam escape or cover is hot to touch — 5–8 minutes.

Remove cover; turn vegetable over once or twice with spoon.

Replace cover; cook over <u>medium</u> heat — about 5 minutes. Turn vegetable over once more.

Replace cover; reduce heat to <u>low</u>; cook 5–10 minutes longer or until vegetable is tender.

To cook frozen vegetables on Controlled Heat Unit, see chart, page 7.

14

FOR THE GOURMET TOUCH: New Method vegetables are delicious simply seasoned with salt and melted butter, but they need not always be served this way.

A good cook will add glamour and interest with a perky sauce, a touch of imagination or a whisper of spice or herbs.

Asparagus or Broccoli—A dollop of Hollandaise sauce topped with a strip of pimento — a **dash** or two of lemon juice added to melted butter — a sprinkling of dry mustard added to a cheese sauce — for asparagus try adding basil, tarragon or thyme to melted butter — for broccoli use curry powder, nutmeg or oregano with the melted butter.

Green Beans — Add diced mushrooms and a dash of nutmeg to melted butter — combine with undiluted cream of mushroom soup, then top with crushed canned French fried onion rings — add basil, chives, oregano, savory or thyme to melted butter — sprinkle Parmesan cheese over buttered beans — slivered almonds lightly browned in butter combined with green beans creates Green Beans Almadine.

Beets — Add sliced little green onions or tiny pickled onions to melted butter — try allspice, basil, ground cloves, dill, tarragon or thyme in melted butter.

Lima Beans — Let some Cheddar Cheese Spread melt down through beans after cooking — add cubed fresh, canned or frozen pineapple chunks for the oriental touch — try a little marjoram in melted butter for a taste that is different.

Carrots — Sprinkle buttered carrots with chopped fresh parsley or mint — like parsnips, small whole carrots can be dipped in beaten egg with milk then in crushed corn flake crumbs and browned in butter — a dash of allspice, basil, chervil, curry powder, ginger or thyme sparks up flavor — carrots can also be glazed or candied like sweet potatoes.

Cauliflower — Add croutons (cubed bread browned in butter) or top with butter — browned dry bread crumbs — try a pinch of basil, rosemary, or curry powder in a dressing of melted butter — caraway seeds or poppy seeds are good additions — stud cooked whole head with slivered almonds.

Spinach — Top with grated hard cooked egg — crumbled crisp cooked bacon and a little bacon drippings give unusual flavor — try a sprinkling of allspice, basil, chervil, oregano or thyme with a melted butter or cream sauce dressing — a French chef will use commercial sour cream blended with a little horseradish and grated onion.

Tomatoes — Basil or celery salt is a must — be different with finely diced green pepper, celery and little green onions, uncooked of course.

Vegetable	Preparation	Approximate No. Minutes on Med. Heat	Approximate No. Minutes on Low Heat
Artichokes	Remove stem, outer leaves. Put into sauce pan. Freshen in cold water 25 minutes. Rinse; drain; cover; cook. Remove choke.	5 min.	30-45 min.
Asparagus	Remove tough lower part of stock; wash. Put into sauce pan; rinse; drain; cover; cook.	5 min.	15-20 min.
Beans, Green or Yellow	Wash; snap off ends; cut into 1-inch pieces or slit lengthwise. Put into sauce pan; rinse; drain; cover; cook.	5 min.	30-35 min.
Beans, Lima	Shell; wash. Put into sauce pan; rinse; drain; cover; cook.	5 min.	25-30 min.

Beets	Remove roots, stems, blemishes; scrub well; slice, dice or leave whole if small. Put into sauce pan; rinse; drain; cover. Cook
	     diced or sliced
	     small whole
		
		5 min.
		5 min.
			
			30-35 min.
			35-40 min.

Beet Greens	Wash well; discard wilted leaves. Put into sauce pan; rinse; drain; cover; cook.	5 min.	12-15 min.
Broccoli	Remove tough outer leaves, lower part of stock; cut lengthwise into pieces. Put into sauce pan; rinse; drain; cover; cook.	5 min.	25-30 min.
Brussels Sprouts	Wash; remove discolored outer leaves. Put into sauce pan. Freshen in cold water 30 minutes if necessary; rinse; drain; cover; cook.	5 min.	25-30 min.
Cabbage	Wash; remove wilted leaves; quarter; core; chop or shred. Put into sauce pan; rinse; drain; cover; cook.	5 min.	20-25 min.

Carrots	Remove tip of root, stem, blemishes; scrub well; slice, dice or leave whole if small. Put into sauce pan; rinse; drain; cover. Cook
	     sliced or diced
	     small whole
		
		5 min.
		5 min.
			
			18-20 min.
			25-30 min.

Cauliflower	Remove leaves; cut off stalk. Score core with six deep crisscross cuts if to be cooked whole or separate into flowerets; wash well. Put into sauce pan, stalks in bottom, flowerets on top; rinse; drain; cover. Cook
	     flowerets
	     whole
		
		5 min.
		5 min.
			
			20 min.
			25 min.

Celery	Cut off root, leaves; separate into stalks; save heart to serve later; remove any coarse strings; dice. Put into sauce pan; rinse; drain; cover; cook.	5 min.	20-25 min.
Corn on the Cob	Remove husks, silk, bad spots; wash inner husks then use to make bed in bottom of sauce pan or broiler pan. Place corn in layers on top, sprinkling each layer lightly with salt. Cover; cook.	5 min.	12-15 min.
Eggplant	Pare; cut into ¼-inch slices. Dip slices in beaten egg and milk, then in dry crumbs. Melt butter in broiler pan; add eggplant; brown on both sides.	10-12 min.	

Vegetable	Preparation	Approximate No. Minutes on Med. Heat	Approximate No. Minutes on Low Heat
Kale	Cut off root, heavy part of stem; discard wilted leaves; wash well. Put into sauce pan; rinse; drain; cover; cook.	5 min.	18-20 min.
Kohlrabi	Cut off top; scrub; slice or quarter. Put into sauce pan; rinse; drain; cover; cook.	5 min.	25-30 min.
Mushrooms	Wash; remove tip of stem; do not peel; slice or leave whole. Put into sauce pan; rinse; drain; cover. Cook sliced whole	 5 min. 5 min.	 8-10 min. 15 min.
Onions	Cut off root, stem end; remove outer skin. Quarter or leave whole. Put into sauce pan; rinse; drain; cover; cook.	5 min.	25-30 min.
Parsnips	Cut off root, stem end; wash, scrub. Put into sauce pan; rinse; drain; cover; cook. Plunge into cold water; slip off skin; brown on all sides in butter in broiler pan.	5 min.	30-35 min.
Peas	Shell peas; wash. Put into sauce pan; rinse; drain; cover; cook.	5 min.	15-18 min.
Potatoes, white	Wash; scrub; remove blemishes. If to be served whole, make crisscross cut on flat side; dry thoroughly. Preheat sauce pan on medium-high heat 5 minutes. Put potatoes in pan; cover; cook. For baked potato: press sides to open cut. For mashed or riced: put through Food Press.	10 min.	40-45 min.
Potatoes, sweet, yams	Scrub; remove blemishes; wash; dry. Put into sauce pan; cover; cook.	5 min.	35-40 min.
Pumpkin	Wash; halve, remove seeds, fiber. Cut into 2-inch pieces; do not peel. Put into sauce pan, skin side down, placing one on top of the other; cover; cook. Put through Food Press.	5 min.	35-45 min.
Rutabaga	Cut off roots, tops; peel thinly; dice. Put into sauce pan; cover; cook.	5 min.	30-35 min.
Spinach	Cut off roots, tough stems; discard wilted leaves; wash well. Put into sauce pan; rinse; drain; cover; cook.	5 min.	10-15 min.
Squash, Summer	Wash; quarter, dice. Put into sauce pan; rinse; drain; cover; cook.	5 min.	10-20 min.
Squash, Winter	Wash; halve; remove seeds, fiber. If large, cut into quarters or eighths. Put into sauce pan, skin side down, placing one on top of other; rinse; drain; cover; cook.	5 min.	20-25 min.
Swiss Chard	Remove wilted leaves; wash; cut leaves and stems. Put into sauce pan; rinse; drain; cover; cook.	5 min.	10-15 min.
Tomatoes	Wash; remove blemishes; quarter. Put into sauce pan; cover; cook.	5 min.	10-15 min.
Turnips	Cut off tops, roots; scrub well; slice or dice. Put into sauce pan; rinse; drain; cover; cook.	5 min.	35-45 min.

LEFTOVER VEGETABLES need never be a problem. To retain flavor, color and freshness, wrap in Alcoa Wrap and store in the refrigerator for use later.

To use "as is" place foil package in pan, add about 1 inch of water, cover and heat 10–15 minutes. Vegetable will taste just like one freshly cooked. One or more packages can be heated at the same time and the pan stays clean.

For a vegetable medley, combine two or more vegetables such as lima beans, celery, carrots, whole grain corn and peas. Add a little chopped pimento for color contrast.

Glorify hamburgers by topping them with gravy to which some leftover vegetables have been added.

Leftover vegetables may be added to many casserole dishes.

Reheated asparagus or broccoli topped with a cheese sauce makes a good side dish.

Many leftover vegetables make good extenders for soups.

HAPPY BLENDINGS

For variety and added interest, try serving vegetables in these combinations:
Peas and diced carrots — peas and diced celery — peas and tiny whole onions.
Diced potatoes and carrots — diced potatoes and celery.
Cubed potatoes and peas nestled in a cream sauce.
Diced turnips and green peppers.
Brussels sprouts, seedless grapes and toasted almonds.
Italian tomatoes cooked whole with sliced zucchini.
Lima beans and whole grain corn.

Vegetable	Characteristics of Good Quality	Number of Servings	Amount to Buy	Pan to Use
Asparagus	Stalks straight, crisp, green; tips moist, compact, unbroken	2 4 6	⅔ pound; 8—10 stalks 1⅓ pounds; 16—20 stalks 2 pounds; 24—30 stalks	781 781½ 782
Beans, Green or Yellow	Pods crisp, bright color, well filled	2 4 6	½ pound 1 pound 1½ pounds	780½ 781 781½
Beans, Lima	Pods clean, unspotted, green, well filled	2 4 6	1—1½ pounds in pod 2—3 pounds in pod 4 pounds in pod	780½ 781 781½
Beets	Young, tops fresh, unwilted; mature; smooth velvety skin	2 4 6	½ pound; 2—4 beets 1 pound; 4—8 beets 1½ pounds; 6—12 beets	780½ 781 781½
Broccoli	Buds dark green, compact; stems short, crisp	2 4 6	⅔ pound 1⅓ pounds 2 pounds	781 781½ 782
Brussels Sprouts	Heads round, solid, compact, green	2 4 6	½ pound 1 pound 1½ pounds; 1 quart	780½ 781 781½
Cabbage	Head solid, heavy; leaves fresh	2 4 6	½ pound 1 pound 1½ pounds	781 781½ 782
Carrots	Firm, uniform shape; bright color; fresh tops	2 4 6	⅔ pound 1⅓ pounds 2 pounds	781 781½ 782
Cauliflower	Head white, well filled; leaves fresh, green	2 4 6	small; 1 pound medium; 1½ pounds large; 2½ pounds	781½ 782 784½
Corn on Cob	Ears well filled; husks green; kernels soft, milky	2 4	2—4 ears 4—8 ears	782 784½
Greens, Kale, Spinach, Swiss Chard	Leaves fresh, crisp, tender	2 4 6	¾ pound 1½ pounds 2½ pounds	781½ 782 784½
Peas	Pods green, unspotted, velvety, well filled	2 4 6	1 pound 2 pounds 3 pounds	780½ 781 781½
Potatoes	Clean, smooth, firm. Regular shape and size	2 4 6	2 medium; ⅔ pound 4 medium; 1⅓ pounds 6 medium; 2 pounds	781 781½ 782
Squash, Summer (Cymling, Crookneck, Straightneck, Vegetable marrow)	Young, firm, thin skinned	2 4 6	small; ½ pound medium; 1 pound large; 1½ pounds	780½ 781 781½
Squash, Winter (Hubbard, Acorn)	Thin skinned; heavy for size	2 4	1 acorn; ¼ Hubbard 2 acorn; ½ Hubbard	781½ 784½
Turnips and Rutabagas	Roots smooth, firm, heavy; size small to medium	2 4 6	⅔ pound 1⅓ pounds 2 pounds	780½ 781 781½

Fabulous Vegetable Recipes

ASPARAGUS A LA KING

- ½ pound fresh asparagus, cut into 1-inch pieces
- 2 tablespoons butter or margarine
- 2 tablespoons flour
- 1 cup milk
- ¼ teaspoon salt
  - Dash pepper
- ½ teaspoon leaf oregano
- 1 cup grated Cheddar cheese
- 2 hard cooked eggs, diced

1. Cook asparagus according to directions on page 16.
2. Melt butter in sauce pan; remove from heat.
3. Add flour; stir; add milk.
4. Cook over low heat, stirring constantly until thickened.
5. Add salt, pepper, oregano, cheese; stir until cheese melts.
6. Add eggs, asparagus; blend well.
7. Serve in patty shells or over chow mein noodles.
8. Three-four servings.

RICED POTATOES

1. Place one or two baked potatoes in food press at a time. Remove any dry crust before ricing; if creamy yellow color is not desirable, skin potatoes before ricing.
2. Add salt with each addition of potatoes.
3. Cut butter into cubes, place on top of riced potatoes, preferably before last potatoes are riced.
4. Serve at once.

BAKED POTATOES

1. Scrub potatoes with stiff brush; remove blemishes. Make a crisscross cut on flat side; dry.
2. Preheat sauce pan over medium-high heat 5 minutes.
3. Put potatoes into heated pan; cover.
4. Reduce heat to medium 10 minutes.
5. Reduce heat to medium-low 40-45 minutes or until done.
6. Press lightly on baked potato to open crisscross slit. Add 1 teaspoon butter, dash of paprika, salt to each. If desired, sprinkle opening with grated cheese, chopped parsley.

CORN CHOWDER

- 3 slices bacon
- ¼ cup minced onion
- 1 pound can cream-style corn
- 2 small potatoes, diced (about 1 cup)
- 2 tablespoons butter or margarine
- ⅛ teaspoon pepper
- 1½ teaspoons salt
- 1 tablespoon sugar
- 1 cup milk
- 1 cup light cream

1. Sauté bacon until crisp; remove from fat; reserve for garnish.
2. Sauté onions in bacon drippings until tender.
3. Combine all ingredients, except bacon, in sauce pan; blend well.
4. Simmer 15 minutes, stirring occasionally.
5. Crumble bacon on top before serving.
6. Six servings.

HOT POTATO SALAD

3 medium potatoes
4 slices bacon, diced
⅓ cup minced onion
2 tablespoons flour
2 tablespoons sugar
½ tablespoon salt
½ teaspoon celery seed
Dash pepper
⅓ cup vinegar
¾ cup water

1. Prepare, cook potatoes according to directions for Baked Potatoes on page 20.
2. Remove thin outside skin from potatoes; slice while hot.
3. Broil diced bacon in 10-inch broiler pan; remove bacon; add to potatoes; drain off fat, reserving 3 tablespoons.
4. Return the 3 tablespoons fat to broiler pan; add onions; cook several minutes until tender.
5. Combine flour, sugar, salt, celery seed, pepper; add to onions; blend thoroughly.
6. Slowly add vinegar, water; cook over low heat until thickened.
7. Return potatoes to broiler pan; blend with sauce; cover.
8. Place over low heat 10-15 minutes.
9. Serve hot; garnish with sprigs of parsley.
10. Four servings.

CANDIED SWEET POTATOES

3 medium sweet potatoes
1 cup brown sugar
¾ teaspoon salt
Dash pepper
3 tablespoons butter or margarine

1. Scrub potatoes with stiff brush; remove blemishes; slice crosswise.
2. Put into 10-inch broiler pan.
3. Mix brown sugar, seasonings; sprinkle over sweet potatoes. Dot with butter; cover.
4. Place over low heat; cook 30 minutes.
5. Remove cover; increase heat to medium last 5 minutes to thicken syrup. Turn potatoes to glaze.
6. Four servings.

HARVARD BEETS

2 pounds beets
1 tablespoon cornstarch
½ cup sugar
¼ cup water
½ cup lemon juice or vinegar
½ teaspoon salt

1. Cook beets according to directions on page 16.
2. Mix cornstarch, sugar, water, lemon juice, salt together; cook 5 minutes.
3. Pour over cooked beets; allow to stand a few minutes before serving.
4. Six servings.

CREOLE STUFFED PEPPERS

6 medium green peppers
2 6½-ounce cans crab meat, drained
2 cups cooked rice
1 cup mayonnaise
2 tablespoons chopped onion
Salt, pepper to taste
Dash Tabasco sauce
2 8-ounce cans tomato sauce

1. Cut tops off peppers; remove seeds, membrane.
2. Precook green peppers in boiling water 5 minutes; drain.
3. Sprinkle inside with salt.
4. Combine crab meat, rice, mayonnaise, onion, salt, pepper, Tabasco sauce.
5. Fill peppers with mixture.
6. Place peppers upright in 8 x 8 x 2-inch pan; pour tomato sauce around peppers.
7. Bake 30 minutes at 350°F.
8. Spoon tomato sauce over peppers before serving.
9. Six servings.

MASHED POTATOES

1. Cook; rice potatoes.
2. To 4 cups riced potatoes, add ½ cup hot milk, 1 tablespoon butter, ½ teaspoon salt.
3. Beat until light; fluffy.
4. Four servings.

Delicious Fruits

T HE habit of serving fruit at every meal is a good one. It is so versatile, that not only does it go over big for a first course and for dessert, but combines well with many other foods in salads and main dishes. Spiced fruits of all kinds make an excellent accompaniment for all kinds of meat and fowl. Aside from being a rich source of vitamins and minerals, fruit provides the touch of tartness and the color contrast that excites the appetite.

HOW TO USE THE FOOD PRESS

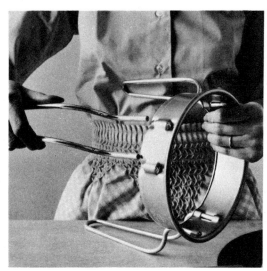

Insert legs into slots in metal collar; drop cone into collar; place bowl beneath cone and set legs on rubber mat.

Fill cone about half way with fruit or vegetables. Place roller in cone, with top of roller in the palm of the hand, fingers extended.

23

With a rolling motion, press vegetables or fruit against side of cone. If food sticks to roller, press it firmly against cone in one spot.

Scrape down wooden roller and outside of cone with a rubber scraper. Discard skins, rinse out cone; wash; rinse and dry thoroughly.

HOW TO COOK FRUITS

1. Select fresh, fully ripe, unspotted fruit. Wash thoroughly; remove stems, blemishes and any soft or bad spots.
2. Follow given recipe. Do not core or peel unless recipe so directs. Place fruit in pan. Best results are obtained when pan is full of fruit. Cover.
3. Place over medium heat until first wisps of steam escape or cover is hot to the touch—about 5 minutes. Reduce heat to low; cook until fruit is done.
4. To cook fruits on Controlled Heat Unit, check the chart on page 7.
5. To make fruit sauces, put through food press as illustrated.

HOW TO COOK BERRIES

1. Select ripe, well colored berries free from white, green or off-color tips.
2. Place berries in food press and wash well by letting water run over them; remove stems. Place in pan. Best results are obtained when pan is full. Cover.
3. Proceed according to instructions 3, 4 and 5 given above for fruits.

SERVING SUGGESTIONS

Peaches, pineapple and apricots are perfect with lamb. Try heating peach or apricot halves, then putting a teaspoon of mint jelly or orange marmalade in the center.

Pineapple slices browned in butter, then sprinkled ever so lightly with curry powder add a different touch.

Cranberries are a must with chicken or turkey and they definitely like keeping company with pork.

When making rhubarb sauce, enhance its flavor and color by cooking strawberries along with the rhubarb.

Just about all fruits go well with beef or veal. Apples, peaches, pineapple and rhubarb are especially good with pork.

For something different; peel ripe bananas and split lengthwise. Roll in lemon juice and sugar. Cook gently in melted butter until golden brown. Serve hot with meat.

Delicious Fruit Recipes

APPLE SAUCE

1. Wash apples; remove stems, blemishes; quarter; do not core.
2. Put into saucepan; cover.
3. Place over <u>medium</u> heat until first wisps of steam escapes or cover is hot to touch—about 5 minutes.
4. Reduce heat to <u>low</u>; cook 10-15 minutes or until soft.
5. Add sugar to taste; cook 5 minutes.
6. Put through food press.

BAKED APPLES

1. Wash; remove cores, blemishes.
2. Score around middle, just enough to cut skin.
3. Put into sauce pan; fill center of each with 1 tablespoon sugar mixed with ¼ teaspoon cinnamon or favorite filling.
4. Make syrup of 4 tablespoons butter or margarine, 1 cup sugar, 1 tablespoon water; pour over apples; cover.
5. Place over <u>low</u> heat; cook 30-40 minutes or until tender.

VARIATION:
Filled apples may be wrapped in foil and placed in sauce pan; cook 25-30 minutes over <u>low</u> heat.

FRUIT CURRY

   ⅓ cup butter or margarine
   ¾ cup light brown sugar, firmly packed
   1 tablespoon curry powder
   1 No. 2 can peach halves, drained
   1 No. 2 can pear haves, drained
   1 No. 2 can pineapple chunks, drained
  12 maraschino cherries, drained

1. Melt butter in 10-inch broiler pan; add brown sugar, curry; blend well.
2. Arrange peaches, pears, pineapple over syrup in pan; place cherries in peach and pear centers; spoon syrup over fruit.
3. Cook covered over <u>low</u> heat 15 minutes; spoon syrup over fruit several times.
4. Serve warm.
5. Six servings.

HOT FRUIT MEDLEY

   2 cups crisp macaroon crumbs (about 40 macaroons)
   1 No. 303 can sliced peaches, drained
   1 1-pound can purple plums, pitted, drained
   1 No. 2 can pineapple chunks, drained
   1 1-pound can Bing Cherries, pitted, drained
  ½ cup Sherry wine

1. Sprinkle ½ cup macaroon crumbs in bottom of buttered 9 x 9 x 1¾-inch pan.
2. Combine peaches, plums, pineapple, cherries; toss lightly.
3. Place layer of fruit in pan; sprinkle with crumbs.
4. Continue layering fruit, crumbs, ending with layer of crumbs.
5. Pour Sherry over top of crumbs.
6. Bake 40-45 minutes at 350°F.
7. Six-eight servings.

CRANBERRY SAUCE

1. Pick over 4 cups cranberries. Wash; drain.
2. Put into sauce pan; cover.
3. Place over low heat; cook 15-20 minutes or until soft.
4. Add 2 cups sugar; cook 5 minutes.
5. Put through food press; mold.

RHUBARB SAUCE

1. Remove tops; wash; do not peel; cut into pieces.
2. Put into sauce pan; cover.
3. Place over medium heat until first wisps of steam escapes or cover is hot to touch—about 5 minutes.
4. Reduce heat to low; cook 15 minutes.
5. Sweeten to taste; cook 5 more minutes.

GRILLED APPLE RINGS

1. Wash; core large cooking apples.
2. Slice into ½-inch thick rings.
3. Dip into flour; broil in 2 tablespoons butter in 10-inch broiler pan.
4. Serve with pork chops or sausage.

Meat -

Fowl - Fish

Down through the centuries meat, fowl and fish have always been well liked foods. They are the heart of the meal—the center around which the menu is planned. There is pleasure associated with eating foods which appeal to the eye and the senses of taste and smell. Meat, fowl or fish present a mouth watering picture and the aroma and flavor tempt even the most jaded appetite.

Aside from looking and tasting good, they are essential in the daily diet as a rich source of the highest quality protein. They furnish valuable amounts of health guarding vitamins and minerals such as iron, copper and phosphorus which go into making of good blood and bones.

Since a large portion of the food budget is spent on these foods, it is wise to know how to cook them properly.

HOW TO ROAST MEATS

Place round roaster over medium-high heat. Explanation of medium-high heat on pages 4 and 5. Put a piece of white paper in pan.

When paper in bottom of pan starts to turn brown, pan is ready to use. Remove paper; reduce heat to medium; place meat in pan.

Brown meat on all sides, allowing about 10 minutes for each side. Meat will stick to hot pan but will loosen as it browns.

Reduce heat to low for the remainder of cooking time. Test for doneness near end of cooking time as given in recipe.

TO ROAST MEATS: Most roasts may be done on top of the range—The Wear-Ever New Method way—without added fat. This is especially recommended for the less tender cuts such as chuck, shoulder, rump or breast of beef. These cuts should be used frequently because they are just as high in food value as the more tender cuts, yet they are less expensive. Pork or veal roasts, small legs of lamb and small hams may also be done the Wear-Ever New Method way.

1.   Place round roaster over <u>medium-high</u> heat. (See explanation of <u>medium-high</u> heat on pages 4 and 5.

2.   Put a small piece of white paper in bottom; when paper <u>starts</u> to turn brown, pan is ready for use. Remove paper; reduce heat to <u>medium</u>; place meat in pan.

3.   Brown meat thoroughly on all sides, allowing about 10 minutes to a side. Meat will stick to hot pan at start, but will loosen itself when sufficiently browned. If meat does not stick to pan, it indicates pan was not hot enough and meat will not brown properly.

4.   Reduce heat to <u>low</u>; season; cover pan with No. 843 cover if roast is small or No. 855 cover if roast is large.

5.   Continue to cook according to time specified in recipe for the kind of roast you are preparing.

6.   To roast on Controlled Heat Unit see chart on page 7.

7.   Following the same procedure, a small roast may be roasted in the 10-inch broiler pan with No. 843 cover.

FROZEN MEATS—FOWL—FISH should be completely thawed, then prepared and cooked the same as fresh meat or fowl. Frozen fish should be thawed just to the point where a few ice crystals remain, then cooked the same as fresh fish.

TO PAN BROIL MEATS means to cook meats the Wear-Ever New Method way without added fat. It is recommended for steaks, chops, ham slices and hamburgers.

1.   Place 10-inch broiler pan over <u>medium-high</u> heat. (See explanation of <u>medium-high</u> heat on pages 4 and 5.

2.   Put a small piece of white paper in pan. When paper <u>starts</u> to turn brown, pan is ready to use. Remove paper.

3.   Place meat in pan; reduce heat to <u>medium</u>. When cold meat hits the hot pan, it will stick just as your warm fingers will adhere to a tray of ice cubes. As the meat browns, it will loosen.

4.   When brown on one side, turn to brown other side. Broil to desired degree of doneness, turning several times if necessary; season.

5.   To pan broil on Controlled Heat Unit see chart on page 7.

6.   If a large quantity of meat is to be pan broiled use the No. 918 utility pan.

Place 10-inch broiler pan over <u>medium-high</u> heat. See explanation for <u>medium-high</u> heat on pages 4 and 5 in front of <u>book</u>.

Place meat in pan; reduce heat to <u>medium</u>. Cold meat will stick, but will loosen as it browns. Turn to brown on both sides.

WEAR-EVER NEW METHOD UTENSILS FOR
MEAT-FOWL-AND FISH

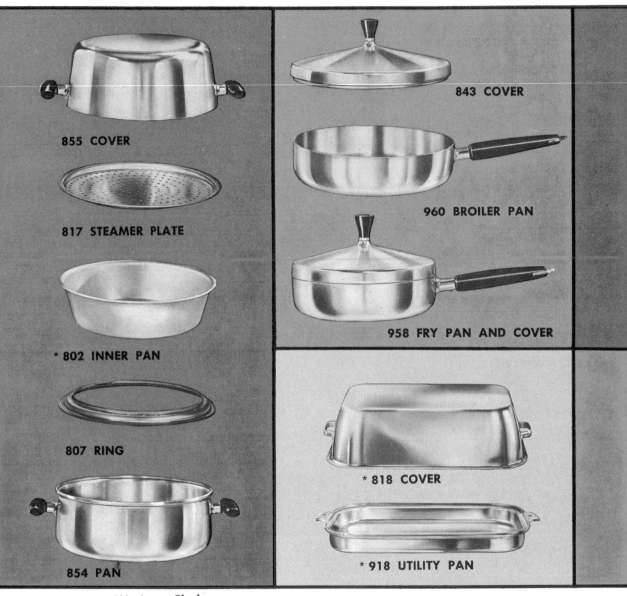

855 COVER

817 STEAMER PLATE

* 802 INNER PAN

807 RING

854 PAN

843 COVER

960 BROILER PAN

958 FRY PAN AND COVER

* 818 COVER

* 918 UTILITY PAN

*No Inner-Clad

WEAR-EVER New Method Utensils can be used in many combinations, thus increasing their usefulness.

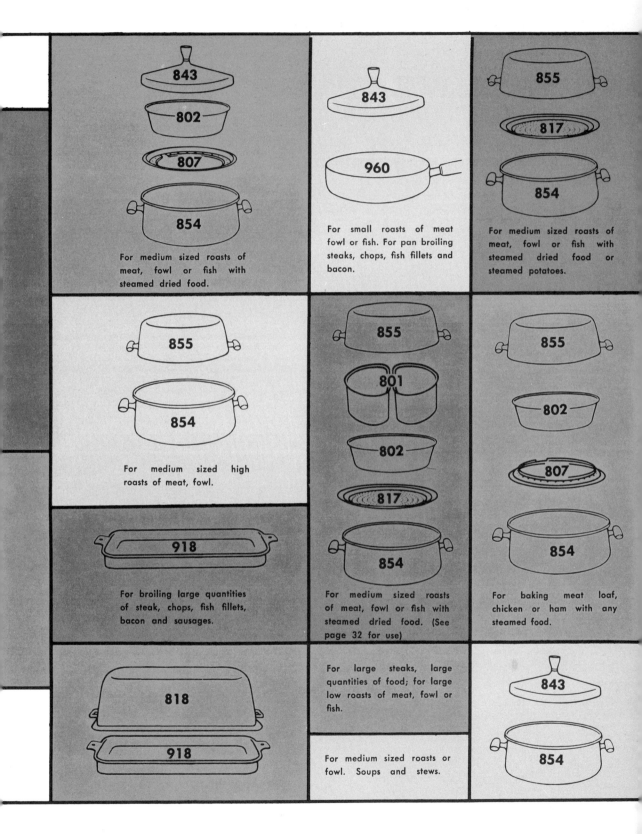

843
802
807
854

For medium sized roasts of meat, fowl or fish with steamed dried food.

843
960

For small roasts of meat fowl or fish. For pan broiling steaks, chops, fish fillets and bacon.

855
817
854

For medium sized roasts of meat, fowl or fish with steamed dried food or steamed potatoes.

855
854

For medium sized high roasts of meat, fowl.

855
801
802
817
854

For medium sized roasts of meat, fowl or fish with steamed dried food. (See page 32 for use)

855
802
807
854

For baking meat loaf, chicken or ham with any steamed food.

918

For broiling large quantities of steak, chops, fish fillets, bacon and sausages.

818
918

For large steaks, large quantities of food; for large low roasts of meat, fowl or fish.

For medium sized roasts or fowl. Soups and stews.

843
854

MEAT, FOWL AND FISH BUYING GUIDE ▬▬▬

Meat	Characteristics of Good Quality	Amount to Allow Per Serving	Pan to Use
Beef	Color purplish brown when first cut, changing rapidly to bright cherry red when exposed to air; lean, firm, fine grained, well marbled with fat; bones red and porous; fat white, brittle, flaked.	Boned and rolled—¼ pound Ground—¼ pound With bone—½ pound Canned, cooked, boneless meats—3 ounces Chipped dried beef—1½ ounces For meat stock—Allow 3 pounds raw meat to 1 gallon stock	Large roasts ...... 854 Small roasts ....960 Large steaks ...... 918 Medium steaks .. 960 Small steaks 958
Veal	Color light greyish pink; lean, firm, fine grained, well marbled with fat; fat white, firm, free from fiber; bones silghtly pink.	Boned and rolled—¼ pound Ground—¼ pound With bone—½ pound	Large roasts ...... 854 Small roasts ....960 Large cutlets ......918 4—8 chops or medium cutlets ....960 1—3 chops 958
Pork (Fresh)	Color light greyish pink; lean, firm, fine grained, well marbled with fat; fat white, firm, free from fibers; bones silghtly pink.	Boned and rolled—¼ pound Ground—¼ pound With bone—½ pound	Large roasts .... 854 Small roasts ....960 Many chops ....918 4—8 chops .... 960 1—3 chops 958
Pork (Smoked)	Color, rich pink; lean, fine grained, well marbled with fat and a good layer of fat on outside; bone small.	Boned and rolled—¼ pound Ground—¼ pound With bone—½ pound Boned and cooked—2-3 ounces Bacon, sliced—2 ounces	Large roasts ....854 Small roasts ....960 2 large steaks ... 918 Average steak 960
Lamb	Color dull pink; lean, firm, fine grained, tender, well marbled with fat; fat firm, white, thin and web-like; bones soft and red.	Boned and rolled—¼ pound Ground—¼ pound With bone—½ pound Meat stock—allow 3 pounds raw meat to 1 gallon stock	Large roasts ....854 Small roasts ....960 Many chops .... 918 4—10 chops ....960 1—3 chops 958
Chicken	Skin smooth, unbroken, moist; legs smooth and soft; fat distributed evenly; breast bone pliable.	Drawn weight— Broilers—1-2 pounds Fryers—1 pound Roasters or Stewers—½-¾ pound	Roasting ....854 Frying ...... 960 or 918
Duck	Breast firm, thick, tender; breastbone and bill pliable.	Drawn weight—1 pound	Roasting 854
Fish (Fresh)	Firm flesh; bright eyes; fresh odor.	Whole—½ pound Fillets—⅓ pound Steaks—⅓ pound	Pan Broiling ....960 or 958

HOW TO COOK A COMPLETE MEAL
IN THE ROUND ROASTER

Vegetables or fruits (fresh, frozen or dried) and the meat for a meal can be prepared—The Wear-Ever New Method Way—at the same time in the round roaster.

1. Follow the instructions TO ROAST MEATS on page 28, using a low roast that fits in the bottom pan.

2. After the meat has been browned, sliced onion may be placed on top for seasoning, then place the No. 817 steamer plate in the pan above the roast.

   a. The vegetables or fruits may be cooked in the No. 801 insert pans or the No. 802 inner pan placed on the steamer plate. Cover pan with No. 855 cover.

   b. Baking potatoes may be cut in half and placed directly on steamer plate above roast.

   c. Cooking time for meat after browning is approximately 25 minutes per pound. Vegetables or fruits may be put on at the same time as meat, but may take less time for cooking.

Meat-Fowl-Fish Recipes

BEEF

PAN BROILED STEAK

1. Trim excess fat, bone from steak.
2. Heat 10-inch broiler pan over medium-high heat until a piece of white paper placed in bottom starts to turn brown.
3. Reduce heat to medium; add meat; brown well on both sides.
4. Turn frequently; continue to cook to desired degree of doneness.
5. Season; serve.

HAMBURGERS

    1 pound beef, ground
    1 large green pepper, chopped
    2 small onions, chopped
      Salt

1. Mix all ingredients together; form into flat cakes.
2. Heat 10-inch broiler pan over medium-high heat until a piece of white paper placed in bottom starts to turn brown.
3. Reduce heat to medium; add meat; brown well on both sides, turning frequently.
4. Four servings.

ROAST BEEF

    Chuck, shoulder, breast, rump roast
    Salt, pepper, paprika

1. Heat round roaster over medium-high heat until a piece of white paper placed in bottom starts to turn brown.
2. Reduce heat to medium; add roast; brown well on all sides—about 20 minutes.
3. Reduce heat to low; cover; roast 25 minutes per pound for medium; 35 minutes per pound for well done.
4. Season near end of cooking time with salt, pepper, paprika.

LIVER AND ONIONS

1. Roll slices of liver in seasoned flour.
2. Sauté in butter in 10-inch broiler pan until brown on both sides.
3. Sauté thinly sliced onion rings in 8-inch fry pan until golden brown.
4. Place liver on platter; turn onion rings into pan in which liver was cooked. Add 2 tablespoons hot water; stir to loosen sediment in pan; mix; pour over liver.

BEEF STROGANOFF

        3 tablespoons butter or margarine
    1/2 pound fresh mushrooms or
            2 4-ounce cans
        1 large onion, cut into 1/2-inch slices
    1 1/2-2 pounds flank steak
        1 tablespoon bottled horseradish
    1/2 cup water
        1 teaspoon thick condiment sauce
    1 1/4 teaspoons salt
    1/8 teaspoon pepper
        1 cup commercial sour cream

1. Melt butter in 10-inch broiler pan; sauté mushrooms, onion slices 5 minutes; remove from fat.
2. Trim fat from steak; mince fat; add to butter in broiler pan.
3. Remove tough, fibrous skin from steak.
4. Slice meat across grain into 1-inch strips; roll in flour; brown on all sides in butter.
5. Place onion-mushroom mixture on top of meat; add horseradish, water, condiment sauce, salt, pepper.
6. Cover; cook over low heat 2 hours or until meat is tender.
7. Just before serving, add sour cream; thicken gravy if desired.
8. Six servings.

SLOPPY JOES

    1/4 cup sliced onions
    1/2 cup diced green pepper
        2 tablespoons fat
        2 medium tomatoes, peeled
    3/4 cup diced mushrooms
    1/2 pound ground beef
        1 cup tomato juice
    1/4 teaspoon paprika
    1/4 teaspoon pepper
    3/4 teaspoon salt

1. Sauté onion, green pepper in fat in 10-inch broiler pan until lightly browned.
2. Cut tomatoes into eighths; add.
3. Add mushrooms, beef, tomato juice, paprika, pepper, salt.
4. Cover; cook over low heat 15-20 minutes.
5. Thicken juice if desired; serve over split toasted buns.
6. Four servings.

SWISS STEAK

    1 1/2 pounds round steak, 1 1/2
            inches thick
        2 tablespoons flour
        1 teaspoon salt
    1/8 teaspoon pepper
        2 tablespoons melted fat
        1 cup hot water
        3 large onions, peeled, sliced

1. Trim excess fat from meat; cut into serving size pieces.
2. Combine flour, salt, pepper.
3. Place meat on breadboard; sprinkle with half of flour mixture; pound it into meat using rim of saucer.
4. Turn meat; pound remaining flour into second side.
5. Melt fat in round roaster over medium heat.
6. Brown meat on both sides.
7. Add water, onions; cover; cook over low heat 1 1/2-2 hours or until meat is tender.
8. More water may be added if necessary during cooking.
9. Four servings.

VARIATIONS:
1. Use 1 1/2 cups canned tomatoes instead of water.
2. Substitute tomato sauce or vegetable juice for all or part of water.
3. Add 2 tablespoons ketchup, 1/2 teaspoon prepared mustard to water.
4. Add 1 green pepper, seeded and cut into thin rings.

STANDING RIB OF BEEF

1. Wipe meat with damp cloth to remove any small loose pieces of bone.
2. Rub meat on all sides with cut side of a clove of garlic.
3. Sprinkle with salt, pepper; do not flour.
4. Place meat fat side up in utility pan or shallow bake pan.
5. Add no water; do not baste; do not cover.
6. Roast a 5-8 lb. rib at 325°F.
        Rare—17-22 minutes per pound
        Medium—22-26 minutes per pound
        Well Done—28-33 minutes per pound

MEAT LOAF

   2 eggs, beaten
1½ pounds ground beef
   ½ pound ground pork
   2 cups soft bread crumbs
   ¾ cup minced onion
   ¼ cup minced green pepper
   2 tablespoons bottled horseradish
   1 tablespoon salt
   ¼ cup milk
   ¼ cup ketchup
   1 teaspoon dry mustard

1. Add eggs to meat; blend lightly.
2. Add remaining ingredients; mix thoroughly but do not stir more than necessary as it tends to toughen loaf.
3. Shape into loaf.
4. This meat may be baked in 10-inch broiler pan or round roaster. Bake over <u>low</u> heat 1 hour.
5. When done, loosen meat loaf from pan with spatula; lift from pan; place on platter.
6. Six servings.

SAUERBRATEN

   3 pounds beef, round or shoulder
   ½ cup vinegar
   ½ cup water
   1 small onion, thinly sliced
   2 bay leaves
   3 whole cloves
   2 teaspoons salt
   ⅛ teaspoon pepper
   4 tablespoons fat
   1 cup water

1. Place meat in bowl.
2. Combine vinegar, water, onion, bay leaves, cloves, salt, pepper; blend.
3. Pour over meat; let stand 18-24 hours.
4. Melt fat in round roaster.
5. Add meat; brown thoroughly on both sides.
6. Add water to liquid in which meat was soaked; pour over meat.
7. Cover; simmer over <u>low</u> heat 3 hours or until meat is tender.
8. Remove meat; make gravy from juices in pan.
9. Six servings.

BEEF STEW

1¾ pounds beef, 1½ inches thick, chuck or round
   ⅓ cup flour
   ¼ teaspoon pepper
   ½ teaspoon salt
   3 tablespoons fat or drippings
   ¼ cup diced onion
   1 minced clove of garlic
2¾ cups boiling water
   1 cup canned tomatoes
   ½ teaspoon salt
   ½ teaspoon Worcestershire sauce
3-4 medium potatoes, pared, quartered
 12 small white onions, peeled
 12 carrots, scrubbed, cut into 2-inch pieces
   1 cup frozen peas (½ pkg.)

1. Trim excess fat from meat; cut into 1½-inch cubes.
2. Combine flour, pepper, salt in paper bag; add meat; shake until pieces are coated.
3. Melt fat in round roaster; add meat; brown on all sides.
4. Add diced onion, garlic, water, tomatoes, salt, Worcestershire sauce.
5. Cover; reduce heat to <u>low</u>; simmer 2 hours or until meat is tender.
6. Add potatoes, onions, carrots; cook 20 minutes.
7. Add peas; cook 15 minutes longer.
8. Four servings.

VARIATIONS:
1. Drop dumplings may be added when peas are put in to cook.
2. Stew may be served over cooked noodles, in which case omit potatoes.
3. Place stew in casserole; top with baking powder biscuits or flaky pastry; bake 20-25 minutes at 450°F.

HUNGARIAN GOULASH WITH NOODLES

  ½ **pound beef, cut into cubes**
  1 **medium onion, minced**
  ⅛ **teaspoon dry mustard**
  ¾ **teaspoon paprika**
  1 **tablespoon brown sugar**
  ½ **teaspoon salt**
1½ **tablespoons Worcestershire sauce**
  ½ **teaspoon cider vinegar**
  3 **tablespoons ketchup**
  ¾ **cup water**
1½ **tablespoons flour**
  3 **ounces uncooked noodles**

1. Brown meat on all sides in 10-inch broiler pan; add onion.
2. Combine mustard, paprika, brown sugar, salt.
3. Combine Worcestershire sauce, vinegar, ketchup; add to mustard mixture; add to meat; add ½ cup of the water; stir; cover.
4. Cook over <u>low</u> heat 2½ hours or until meat is very tender.
5. Blend flour with remaining ¼ cup water; add to meat mixture; stir until thickened.
6. Cook noodles in salted water until tender; drain.
7. Serve meat mixture over noodles.
8. Four servings.

BEEF ROLI POLI

PART ONE:
1½ **tablespoons fat**
  ½ **pound beef, ground or**
  1 **cup ground leftover beef**
  ½ **cup chopped mushrooms**
  ½ **medium onion, minced**
  1 **egg, beaten**
  ¾ **teaspoon salt**
    Dash pepper
  ½ **tablespoon minced parsley**

1. Melt fat in 10-inch broiler pan; add meat, mushrooms, onions; cook until brown, stirring occasionally.
2. Add egg, salt, pepper, parsley; mix well; set aside to cool.

PART TWO:
1½ **cups sifted all purpose flour**
2¼ **teaspoons baking powder**
  ½ **teaspoon salt**
  1 **tablespoon sugar**
  ¼ **cup shortening**
  ½ **cup milk**

1. Sift dry ingredients together; cut in shortening; add milk to make a soft dough.
2. Roll on lightly floured board to ½-inch thickness.
3. Spread with meat mixture; roll up as for jelly roll.
4. Cut into 1-inch slices; place in shallow baking pan; brush with butter.
5. Bake 20-25 minutes at 425°F.
6. Serve with a sauce made by adding ½ cup leftover cooked vegetables to 1½ cups mushroom soup or to equal amount of gravy.
7. Four servings.

BRAISED SHORT RIBS OF BEEF

  2 **pounds beef short ribs, cut into 3-inch pieces**
  1 **clove garlic, peeled, cut in half**
  2 **tablespoons flour**
  2 **teaspoons salt**
  ½ **teaspoon pepper**
  2 **tablespoons fat**
1½ **cups boiling water**
  1 **large onion, sliced**

1. Lightly rub short ribs with cut side of garlic.
2. Combine flour, salt, pepper.
3. Coat meat with flour mixture.
4. Melt fat in 10-inch broiler pan; add meat; brown on all sides.
5. Add water, sliced onions.
6. Cover; cook over <u>low</u> heat 2 hours or until meat is loosened from bones.
7. Four servings.

DELICIOUS MEAT BALLS

  1 **pound round beef, ground twice**
  ½ **pound pork tenderloin, ground**
  3 **eggs, beaten**
  1 **teaspoon salt**
  ⅛ **teaspoon pepper**
  2 **tablespoons flour**
  ¼ **cup salad oil or shortening**
 1½ **tablespoons flour**
  1 **10½-ounce can condensed beef**
      consommé, undiluted
  ½ **tablespoon bottled sauce for gravy**
  ½ **cup Sherry wine**

1. Combine ground beef, pork, beaten eggs, salt, pepper, flour; toss together lightly.
2. Heat salad oil in 10-inch broiler pan.
3. Shape meat into small balls, ¾ to 1-inch in diameter.
4. Brown, a few at a time, in hot fat; remove each ball as soon as it is well browned.
5. When browning is complete, add remaining flour to fat in broiler pan; stir until smooth.
6. Add consommé, bottled sauce; cook, stirring constantly until thickened.
7. Add Sherry; blend; pour over meat balls in serving dish.
8. Six servings.

CHILI CON CARNE

  1 **tablespoon butter or margarine**
  1 **pound ground beef**
  ½ **cup diced onion**
  1 **No. 2 can red kidney beans**
  2 **cups tomato soup**
  1 **teaspoon salt**
  ¼ **teaspoon chili powder**

1. Melt butter in 10-inch broiler pan; add meat, onion; cook until brown; stir frequently.
2. Add remaining ingredients; stir; cover.
3. Cook over <u>low</u> heat 20-25 minutes; stir occasionally.
4. Four servings.

ROAST BEEF HASH

  3 **tablespoons butter or margarine**
  2 **tablespoons minced onion**
  3 **tablespoons flour**
 1½ **cups beef stock or left-over gravy**
  ½ **teaspoon bottled meat sauce**
  ½ **teaspoon dried parsley**
  ¼ **teaspoon salt**
  ⅛ **teaspoon pepper**
  3 **cups ground cooked beef**
  2 **cups finely diced cooked potatoes**
  2 **tablespoons butter or margarine**
  2 **cups soft bread crumbs**

1. Melt butter in 10-inch broiler pan; add onion; cook until lightly browned.
2. Blend in flour, stock; bring to boil.
3. Blend in bottled meat sauce, parsley, salt, pepper, meat, potatoes.
4. Spoon into 1½-quart casserole.
5. Melt butter; add bread crumbs; toss; place on top of mixture.
6. Bake uncovered 30 minutes at 350°F.
7. Four servings.

LEFTOVER DAYS

To retain flavor and freshness, wrap leftover roast beef in Alcoa Wrap and store in refrigerator for use later. To serve "as is", place foil package in shallow pan; heat 20–25 minutes at 400°F. May also be reheated on steamer plate over boiling water in round roaster.

Slice roast; heat in gravy in 10-inch broiler pan for hot roast beef sandwiches.

Ground leftover beef blended with a little pickle relish and mayonnaise makes a good lunch box sandwich filling.

Our Roast Beef Hash, page 37, is just about the best you ever tasted.

Chili Con Carne, page 37; Sloppy Joes, page 34, and Beef Roli Poli, page 36 use up the last of the roast, ground of course, and only you will know.

LAMB

PAN BROILED LAMB CHOPS

1. Remove excess fat from chops.
2. Heat 10-broiler pan over <u>medium-high</u> heat until a piece of white paper placed in bottom starts to turn brown.
3. Reduce heat to <u>medium</u>; add meat; brown well on both sides.
4. Turn frequently; continue to cook until done.
5. Season; serve.

ROAST LEG OF LAMB

1. Have butcher cut off bone at first joint; french; skewer; wipe.
2. Remove fell; rub with garlic.
3. Heat round roaster over <u>medium-high</u> heat until a piece of white paper placed in bottom starts to turn brown.
4. Reduce heat to <u>medium</u>; add meat; brown well on all sides.
5. Reduce heat to <u>low</u>; cover; cook 30-35 minutes per pound.
6. Season with salt, pepper near end of cooking time.
7. Serve with mint sauce or use one of the Glazes for Roast Lamb.
8. Eight servings.
NOTE: Lamb Shoulder may be prepared same way.

GLAZES FOR ROAST LAMB

CURRY-PINEAPPLE GLAZE
1 teaspoon curry powder
1 flat can crushed pineapple (1 cup)

1. Combine all ingredients; blend well; spoon over lamb near end of cooking time.

HERB-BUTTER GLAZE
6 tablespoons butter or margarine, softened
1½ teaspoons salt
½ teaspoon garlic salt
¼ teaspoon coarse-ground pepper
1 tablespoon lemon juice

1. Combine all ingredients; blend well; spoon over lamb near end of cooking time.

HONEY-MUSTARD GLAZE
¼ cup prepared mustard
¼ cup honey
½ teaspoon salt
⅛ teaspoon pepper

1. Combine all ingredients; blend well; spoon over lamb near end of cooking time.

ORANGE MARMALADE GLAZE
½ cup orange marmalade
⅓ cup lemon juice
1 teaspoon rosemary leaves
¼ cup finely chopped parsley

1. Combine all ingredients; blend well; spoon over lamb near end of cooking time.

MAGGIE'S LAMB CHOPS

4 loin lamb chops, 1 inch thick
Salt, pepper
4 slices American cheese
4 slices Bermuda onion
½ cup commercial sour cream

1. Wrap tail end of each chop around thick part to form a flat round patty; fasten with toothpicks.
2. Sprinkle with salt, pepper.
3. Place chops in shallow baking pan.
4. Place one slice cheese, one slice onion on each chop.
5. Put 2 tablespoons sour cream on each chop.
6. Add no water; do not cover.
7. Bake 1 hour at 375°F.
8. Four servings.

LAMB CURRY

      2 tablespoons butter or margarine
    ¾ cup sliced onions
      1 cup diced celery
      1 minced clove garlic
    1½ cups cubed cooked lamb
      1 teaspoon curry powder
      2 cups stock or lamb gravy
         Salt
      2 tablespoons flour
    ¼ cup cold water

1. Melt butter in 10-inch broiler pan; sauté onion, celery, garlic in butter until lightly browned.
2. Add lamb, curry powder, stock, salt; cover; simmer over low heat 30 minutes.
3. Make paste from flour, water; stir into curry to thicken; simmer 5 minutes uncovered.
4. Serve over fluffy rice.
5. Four servings.

DORIS' LAMB CHOPS

      2 hard cooked eggs, shelled
    ½ cup butter or margarine
      6 tablespoons fine dry bread crumbs
      2 teaspoons minced onion
      1 teaspoon salt
    ¼ teaspoon pepper
      1 teaspoon Worcestershire sauce
      4 loin lamb chops, 1 inch thick

1. Chop whites of eggs fine; rub yolks through sieve.
2. Melt butter in 10-inch broiler pan; add crumbs, onion; cook over low heat until lightly browned.
3. Add salt, pepper, Worcestershire sauce, eggs; blend well.
4. Sprinkle chops with salt, pepper.
5. Pat crumb mixture on one side of each chop; place a square of Alcoa Wrap on top; turn; pat mixture on second side.
6. Wrap foil around each chop.
7. Place in shallow baking pan; add no water; do not cover.
8. Bake 1 hour at 375°F.
9. To serve: unwrap chops; place on platter; garnish with spiced peaches, parsley.
10. Four servings.

IRISH STEW WITH FLUFFY DUMPLINGS

    1½ pounds lamb shoulder (cut into
         small pieces)
    ½ cup cooked carrots
    ¼ cup cooked turnips
      2 cups cooked potatoes

1. Heat round roaster over medium-high heat until a piece of white paper placed in bottom starts to turn brown.
2. Reduce heat to medium; add meat; brown well on all sides.
3. Add water to cover; bring to boil; reduce heat to low. Cover; cook 2 hours.
4. Twenty minutes before serving add vegetables, sufficient water to make 3 cups liquid. Season with salt.
5. Prepare Fluffy Dumplings; drop on stew; cover; cook 15 minutes.
6. Cover should not be removed until dumplings are ready to serve.
7. Four servings.

FLUFFY DUMPLINGS

Sift together 1 cup all purpose flour, 2 teaspoons baking powder, 1 teaspoon salt. Beat 1 egg; add ½ cup milk, 2 tablespoons melted butter. Add to flour mixture; beat until smooth. Drop from tablespoon on top of stew.

LEFTOVER DAYS

Roast lamb may be reheated the same as roast beef, page 37.
Cubed roast lamb combined with cooked carrots, potatoes, peas and gravy, then topped with biscuits or pie crust and baked, makes an excellent lamb pot pie.
Heat sliced roast lamb in gravy for hot roast lamb sandwiches.
For lamb and potato patties, combine ground leftover lamb with leftover mashed potatoes, a little grated onion, salt, pepper. Shape into patties; roll in flour; brown both sides in melted butter.
Lamb Curry will take care of the last bits and pieces. Use our recipe on page 39.

PORK

PORK CHOPS

1. Trim excess fat from chops.
2. Heat 10-inch broiler pan over medium-high heat until a piece of white paper placed in bottom starts to turn brown.
3. Reduce heat to medium; add meat; brown well on both sides; cover.
4. Reduce heat to low; cook 35-45 minutes or until tender.
5. Season; serve.

PAN BROILED HAM

1. Trim excess fat from ham slice.
2. Heat 10-inch broiler pan over medium-high heat until a piece of white paper placed in bottom starts to turn brown.
3. Reduce heat to medium; add meat; brown well on both sides.
4. Turn frequently; continue to cook until done.

SAUSAGE

1. Prick skins to prevent bursting.
2. Heat 10-inch broiler pan over medium-high heat until a piece of white paper placed in bottom starts to turn brown.
3. Reduce heat to medium; add meat; brown well on all sides; cover.
4. Reduce heat to low; cook 15-20 minutes or until tender.
5. Serve at once.

BARBECUED SPARERIBS

  4 **pounds spareribs**
  1 **clove garlic**
  1 **large onion, diced**
  2 **tablespoons butter or margarine**
  1 **cup canned tomatoes**
  1 **cup diced celery**
  1 **cup diced green pepper**
  1 **cup ketchup**
  2 **tablespoons brown sugar**
  3 **dashes Tabasco sauce**
 ½ **teaspoon dry mustard**
  2 **cups beef stock or 2 bouillon cubes dissolved in 2 cups boiling water**
    Salt, pepper

1. Rub ribs with cut side of clove of garlic.
2. Place in shallow baking pan; roast uncovered 30 minutes at 350°F.
3. Brown onion in melted butter in 10-inch broiler pan.
4. Add remaining ingredients; stir; cover.
5. Simmer over low heat 1 hour.
6. After ribs have roasted the 30 minutes, pour sauce over top.
7. Roast 45 minutes longer, basting frequently.
8. Four servings.

BAKED HAM

  4 **pounds ham, butt end**
  4 **tablespoons brown sugar**
10 **whole cloves**

1. Wipe ham with damp cloth; remove brown spots caused by curing.
2. Heat round roaster over medium-high heat until a piece of white paper placed in bottom starts to turn brown.
3. Reduce heat to medium; add meat; brown on all sides; turn fat side up.
4. Reduce heat to low; cover with No. 855 cover; cook 30 minutes.
5. Score fat side with diagonal cuts to form diamonds; insert a clove in center of each diamond; pat brown sugar over surface.
6. Cover; cook 30 minutes longer.
7. Six servings.
NOTE: For special occasions omit point 5. Top with one of the following glazes; bake last 30 minutes in 350°F. oven.

TO GLAZE BAKED HAM

1. Cook ham according to recipe.
2. Remove rind; score or cut fat into squares or diamonds.
3. Insert whole clove into center of each diamond.
4. Spread or baste with one of the following:

> ½ cup canned crushed pineapple combined with ½ cup brown sugar
>
> Pat brown sugar over ham; drizzle on honey or molasses
>
> ½ cup brown sugar mixed with juice and grated rind of ½ orange
>
> ½ cup currant jelly or canned whole cranberry sauce, beaten with fork
>
> ½ cup orange, or orange grapefruit marmalade, beaten with fork
>
> ½ cup brown sugar combined with ½ cup juice from spiced or pickled peaches
>
> 1 cup pureed applesauce, apricots or peaches
>
> ½ cup brown sugar mixed with ½ teaspoon dry mustard, 1 tablespoon vinegar, fruit juice or cider or 1 teaspoon horseradish
>
> ½ cup brown sugar combined with ¼ cup fine soft bread crumbs

Pat brown sugar over ham; place drained pineapple slices on top and maraschino cherry in center of each slice. Fruit may be fastened to ham with toothpicks and removed before serving. Use pineapple juice for basting.

Pat brown sugar over ham. Arrange canned sliced peaches on ham to resemble black eyed daisies. Make centers with small clusters of whole cloves. Use juice for basting.

Canned pineapple juice, cider, canned fruit nectar, corn syrup, Muscatel or Tokay wine may be used for basting.

PAN BROILED BACON

1. Place bacon in cold 10-inch broiler pan.
2. Place over <u>low</u> heat.
3. Turn frequently; drain off excess fat during browning.
4. Cook until crisp; drain on paper.

ROAST CANADIAN BACON

> 1½ pounds Canadian bacon
> Whole cloves
> ⅓ cup brown sugar
> 1½ tablespoons prepared mustard
> 1 cup canned pineapple juice

1. Remove casing from Canadian bacon.
2. Score fat side with sharp knife; stud with cloves.
3. Combine sugar, mustard to make paste; spread over meat.
4. Place in round roaster; pour pineapple juice around sides; cover.
5. Roast over <u>low</u> heat 1 hour.
6. Six servings.

ROAST LOIN OF PORK

1. Wipe 3 pound loin of pork.
2. Heat round roaster over <u>medium-high</u> heat until a piece of white paper placed in bottom starts to turn brown.
3. Reduce heat to <u>medium</u>; add meat; brown well on all sides.
4. Turn fat side up; season.
5. Roast over <u>low</u> heat; cover with No. 855 cover; allow 30-35 minutes per pound.
6. Six servings.

GLAZED HAM BALLS

> ½ pound ground ham
> ½ pound ground pork
> ⅓ cup cracker crumbs
> 1 egg, beaten
> 1 cup evaporated milk
> ⅛ teaspoon salt
> ⅛ teaspoon thyme
> 2 tablespoons minced onion
> ½ cup brown sugar, firmly packed
> ½ teaspoon dry mustard
> 1½ tablespoons vinegar

1. Combine ham, pork, cracker crumbs, egg, evaporated milk, salt, thyme, onion; blend thoroughly.
2. Shape into 8 balls about 2 inches in diameter; place in 9 x 9 x 1¾-inch pan.
3. Combine brown sugar, mustard, vinegar in sauce pan; cook over <u>medium-high</u> heat until boiling; pour over ham balls.
4. Bake uncovered 1 hour at 350°F.
5. Four servings.

SWEET-SOUR PORK

1½ pounds leftover pork, sliced
½ cup water
⅓ cup vinegar
¼ cup brown sugar
2 tablespoons cornstarch
½ teaspoon salt
1 No. 2 can pineapple chunks
1 medium green pepper, thinly sliced
2 medium onions, thinly sliced

1. Brown meat lightly in melted fat in 10-inch broiler pan.
2. In sauce pan combine water, vinegar, sugar, cornstarch, salt, 1 cup pineapple juice drained from chunks.
3. Cook over <u>low</u> heat until clear, slightly thickened.
4. Pour sauce over meat; cover; cook over <u>low</u> heat 30 minutes.
5. Add pineapple chunks, green pepper, onion; cook 2 minutes longer.
6. Serve with fried rice.
7. Four servings.

UPSIDE DOWN PARTY HAM LOAF

1¼ pounds cured ham, ground
¾ pound lean fresh pork, ground
1 cup cracker crumbs
2 eggs, beaten slightly
¾ cup milk
2 tablespoons mustard
3 tablespoons brown sugar
6 pineapple slices, well drained
6 maraschino cherries

1. Mix well all ingredients except brown sugar, pineapple, cherries.
2. Sprinkle brown sugar in 10-inch broiler pan; arrange pineapple rings; place a cherry in center of each ring.
3. Pat ham loaf mixture over entire surface of pineapple; cover.
4. Place over <u>medium</u> heat until cover becomes hot to touch.
5. Reduce heat to <u>low</u>; cook 1 hour.
6. When done, tilt cover, drain off all excess liquid in bottom of pan.
7. Remove cover; place meat platter over meat loaf; invert pan.
8. Eight servings.

STUFFED SPARE RIBS

2 pounds spare ribs
1½ cups bread cubes
1 medium onion, minced
2 tablespoons chopped parsley
1 tablespoon melted butter or margarine
½ teaspoon salt
⅛ teaspoon pepper
1 tablespoon water

1. Wipe meat; sprinkle with salt.
2. Mix bread, onion, parsley, melted butter, seasonings, water together.
3. Spread over spare ribs; roll; fasten with skewers; tie with string.
4. Heat round roaster over <u>medium-high</u> heat until a piece of white paper placed in bottom starts to turn brown.
5. Reduce heat to <u>medium</u>; add meat; brown well on all sides.
6. Reduce heat to <u>low</u>; cover; cook 1½ hours.
7. Four servings.

PORK TURKEYS

4 double loin pork chops (cut about ¾-inch thick)
1½ cups bread cubes
3 tablespoons butter or margarine, melted
½ small onion, minced
¼ teaspoon Worcestershire sauce
¼ teaspoon salt
Dash pepper
3 tablespoons ketchup

1. Have butcher cut pocket in each chop.
2. Make dressing of bread, butter, onion, seasonings. Do not put ketchup in dressing. Place dressing in pocket of each chop. Close openings.
3. Heat 10-inch broiler pan over <u>medium-high</u> heat until a piece of white paper placed in bottom starts to turn brown.
4. Reduce heat to <u>medium</u>; add meat; brown well on both sides.
5. Pour ketchup over top.
6. Reduce heat to <u>low</u>; cover; cook 1 hour.
7. Four servings.

SWEET 'N' SOUR SAUSAGE

       1 pound loose sausage meat
       1 cup pineapple tidbits, drained
       1 cup green pepper strips, about 2
           inches long
       1 cup thinly sliced onion
       ½ cup vinegar
       ⅔ cup syrup from pineapple tidbits
       ½ cup brown sugar
       2 teaspoons soy sauce
       2 small tomatoes, cut in wedges
       2 tablespoons cornstarch
       2 tablespoons cold water

1. Shape sausage into 1-inch balls; place in cold 10-inch broiler pan.
2. Brown meat balls on all sides; spoon off excess grease.
3. Add pineapple, green pepper, onion; brown lightly.
4. Combine vinegar, syrup, brown sugar, soy sauce; pour over meat mixture; add tomatoes; cover.
5. Cook over low heat 20-30 minutes or until no trace of pink remains in center of meat balls.
6. Dissolve cornstarch in water; add to sauce; cook until thickened—about 5 minutes.
7. Serve over rice.
8. Four-six servings.

SAUERKRAUT AND PORK

1. Have bone broken in center of 2 pound loin roast.
2. Heat round roaster over medium-high heat until a piece of white paper placed in bottom starts to turn brown.
3. Reduce heat to medium; add meat; brown well on all sides.
4. Reduce heat to low; cover; cook 2 hours.

SAUERKRAUT

1. Peel, dice ½ small onion.
2. Mix with 1 pound sauerkraut.
3. Place in No. 802 pan on steamer plate over pork roast.
4. Cook 1 hour 15 minutes.
5. Four servings.

PORK CHOPS PIERRE

       ½ tablespoon butter or margarine
       2 tablespoons finely chopped onion
       2 tablespoons finely chopped celery
       2 tablespoons water
       ¼ cup ketchup
       1 tablespoon vinegar
       ½ tablespoon lemon juice
       ½ tablespoon Worcestershire sauce
       ½ tablespoon brown sugar
       ¼ teaspoon salt
         Dash pepper
       4 loin pork chops cut ½-inch thick
       1 medium onion, sliced thin
       1 medium green pepper, cut into rings

1. Melt butter in sauce pan; add onion, celery; cook over low heat until tender.
2. Add water, ketchup, vinegar, lemon juice, Worcestershire sauce, sugar, salt, pepper; cover; simmer 20 minutes.
3. Brown pork chops on both sides in 10-inch broiler pan.
4. Make 4 double-thick squares of Alcoa Wrap.
5. Pour 1 tablespoon of the sauce in the center of each square; place pork chops on top; place 2 slices onion, 1 tablespoon sauce, 2 green pepper rings on top of each chop.
6. Bring torn edges together over meat; fold, then fold again, bringing fold down close to meat. Fold ends over and over pressing in close to meat.
7. Place packages in shallow pan.
8. Bake 45-50 minutes at 425°F.
9. Four servings.

LEFTOVER DAYS

Roast pork or baked ham may be reheated the same as roast beef, page 37.
Sliced roast pork may be heated in gravy for hot roast pork sandwiches.
Combine cubed roast pork and hard cooked eggs, cut in eighths, with condensed cream of mushroom soup. Add a dash of salt, pepper, Worcestershire sauce and heat over low heat. Serve over rice or hot biscuits.
Sweet-Sour Pork Slices, page 42, is an excellent way to serve the last of the roast.
Leftover baked ham is good either reheated or served cold.

VEAL

SWEETBREADS

1. Combine ¼ cup flour, ½ teaspoon salt, ½ teaspoon pepper in clean paper bag.
2. Wash sweetbreads; trim; drop into bag; shake to coat with flour.
3. Melt 3 tablespoons butter or margarine in 10-inch broiler pan over <u>medium</u> heat; add sweetbreads; brown on both sides; cover.
4. Reduce heat to <u>low</u>, cook 10 minutes.

ROAST VEAL

1. Heat round roaster over <u>medium-high</u> heat until a piece of white paper placed in bottom starts to turn brown.
2. Reduce heat to <u>medium</u>; add roast; brown well on all sides—about 20 minutes.
3. Reduce heat to <u>low</u>; cover; roast 35-40 minutes per pound or until meat is fork tender.
4. Season near end of cooking time with salt, pepper, paprika.

NOTE: If desired, strips of bacon may be placed over meat after browning for added flavor.

VEAL STEAK

1. Heat 10-inch broiler pan over <u>medium-high</u> heat until a piece of white paper placed in bottom starts to turn brown.
2. Reduce heat to <u>medium</u>; add meat; brown well on both sides; cover.
3. Reduce heat to <u>low</u>; cook 20-25 minutes or until tender.
4. Season; serve.

VEAL CHOPS

1. Heat 10-inch broiler pan over <u>medium-high</u> heat until a piece of white paper placed in bottom starts to turn brown.
2. Reduce heat to <u>medium</u>; add meat; brown well on both sides; cover.
3. Reduce heat to <u>low</u>; cook 20-25 minutes or until tender.
4. Season; serve.

VEAL PAPRIKA

  2 pounds veal shoulder boned, rolled, tied
  1 tablespoon butter or margarine
  ½ tablespoon paprika
  2 tablespoons flour
  ½ teaspoon salt
  1 tablespoon shortening
  1 small onion, minced
  ½ cup finely diced celery
  2 tablespoons water
  1 tablespoon flour
  ¼ cup commercial sour cream

1. Heat round roaster over <u>medium-high</u> heat until piece of white paper placed in bottom starts to turn brown.
2. Reduce heat to <u>medium</u>; add meat; brown well on all sides.
3. Cream butter; add paprika, flour, salt to make a paste; spread over browned meat.
4. Cover; cook over <u>low</u> heat 1 hour.
5. Melt shortening in 8-inch fry pan; add onion; cook until lightly browned; add celery, water; cover; cook 8-10 minutes.
6. After veal has cooked 1 hour, pour onion-celery mixture over top; cook 1 hour longer or until meat is tender.
7. Stir flour into cream; combine with juice in pan; spoon over veal; cover; cook 15 minutes longer.
8. Four servings.

BRAISED STUFFED BREAST OF VEAL

3½ pounds breast of veal with pocket
2 cups fine bread crumbs
1 small onion, minced
½ cup diced celery
2 tablespoons butter or margarine
¼ cup water
¼ cup grated cheese
1 teaspoon salt
⅛ teaspoon pepper

1. Wipe meat with damp cloth.
2. Mix all ingredients well.
3. Fill pocket; skewer; lace with cord.
4. Heat round roaster over medium-high heat until a piece of white paper placed in bottom starts to turn brown.
5. Reduce heat to medium; add meat; brown well on all sides.
6. Reduce heat to low; cover with No. 855 cover; cook 2 hours.
7. Six servings.

VEAL SCALLOPINI

6 thin slices veal shank
6 tablespoons flour
4 tablespoons butter or margarine
3 medium onions, sliced thin
1 clove garlic, minced
2 bouillon cubes
1 cup boiling water
1 teaspoon dry mustard
3 teaspoons paprika
3 tablespoons minced parsley
4 tablespoons butter or margarine
1 cup commercial sour cream

1. Dust veal with flour.
2. Melt butter in 10-inch broiler pan; add onions, garlic; sauté until tender.
3. Add bouillon cubes, water; stir until cubes dissolve; add mustard, paprika, parsley; stir; pour into bowl; set aside.
4. Melt remaining butter in broiler pan; add floured meat; brown on both sides over medium heat.
5. Pour onion mixture over meat; cover; cook over low heat 30 minutes.
6. Stir in cream; bring to boil; remove from heat.
7. Four servings.

BREADED VEAL CUTLET

2 pounds veal cutlet, ½ inch thick
1 cup dry bread crumbs
½ teaspoon salt
⅛ teaspoon pepper
1 egg, beaten
¼ cup milk
4 tablespoons butter or margarine

1. Cut veal into serving pieces.
2. Combine crumbs, salt, pepper.
3. Combine egg, milk.
4. Dip veal into crumbs, then into egg mixture and into crumbs again.
5. Place breaded veal in refrigerator 30 minutes.
6. When ready to use, melt fat in 10-inch broiler pan.
7. Add meat; cook over low heat about 15 minutes on each side until browned.
8. Four servings.
VARIATIONS:
1. Pour can of tomato sauce over meat after browning; cover; simmer 15 minutes.
2. Pour can of mushroom, celery or chicken soup over meat after browning; cover; simmer 15 minutes.
3. Spoon one pint commercial sour cream over meat after browning; cover; simmer 5 minutes.
4. Brush veal with French dressing before dipping into crumb-egg mixture.
5. Rub veal with cut side of clove of garlic before breading.
NOTE: Veal Chops may be prepared the same way.

LEFTOVER DAYS

Sliced roast veal may be reheated in veal gravy for hot roast veal sandwiches.
Ground leftover veal, blended with a little pickle relish and mayonnaise, makes a good lunch box sandwich filling.
Cubed roast veal, combined with cooked peas, potatoes, carrots and gravy, spiced with a bit of onion and Worcestershire sauce, then topped with biscuits or pie crust and baked, makes a good veal pot pie.
Roast veal may be reheated the same as roast beef, page 37.

FOWL

ROAST CHICKEN

1. Clean; wash; pat dry inside and out; rub inside with salt.
2. Stuff body and neck cavities with desired stuffing; do not pack too tightly as stuffing swells.
3. Skewer openings; lace with cord.
4. Twist wings back and tuck under shoulders to hold wings close to body.
5. Tie legs together with cord; fasten to rump.
6. Spread bird with softened butter, margarine or chicken fat.
7. Heat round roaster over <u>medium-high</u> heat until a piece of white paper placed in bottom starts to turn brown.
8. Reduce heat to <u>medium</u>; add chicken; brown well on all sides, turning frequently; season with salt, pepper.
9. Turn breast side down; reduce heat to <u>low</u>; cover with No. 855 cover.
10. Roast 20-30 minutes per pound or until thigh is tender; turn several times during roasting.

FRIED CHICKEN

1. Select fryer or roaster; cut into desired pieces; wash well; pat dry.
2. Heat round roaster or 10-inch broiler pan over <u>medium</u> heat.
3. Dip pieces into flour, crumbs or batter or leave plain.
4. To flour or crumb: put flour or fine cracker crumbs, seasonings into clean paper bag. Drop pieces of chicken into bag; close opening; shake until chicken is coated.
5. Brown chicken on all sides in a little chicken fat, butter or margarine; season; sprinkle with paprika.
6. If further cooking of chicken is required to make it tender, cover; reduce heat to <u>low</u>; cook 35-40 minutes longer.

CHICKEN MARYLAND

    1 frying chicken
    ¾ teaspoon salt
    ¼ teaspoon pepper
    ¾ cup dry bread crumbs
    1 egg, well beaten
    ¼ cup shortening
    1½ tablespoons flour
    ½ teaspoon salt
    ⅛ teaspoon pepper
    ¾ cup milk

1. Singe; clean; cut up chicken.
2. Mix seasonings, crumbs.
3. Dip into beaten egg; roll in seasoned crumbs.
4. Melt shortening in round roaster over <u>medium</u> heat; add chicken; cover.
5. Reduce heat to <u>low</u>; cook approximately 45 minutes. Turn occasionally to insure even browning.
6. Remove chicken; make gravy by adding flour, salt, pepper, milk to pan.
7. Strain gravy through food press; serve over rice.
8. Four servings.

CHICKEN WITH PEACH SAUCE

    ¾ cup orange juice
    1½ cups canned peach slices
    ⅓ cup syrup from peaches
    2 tablespoons brown sugar
    1 tablespoon vinegar
    ¼ teaspoon dried basil, crushed
    1½ teaspoons mace
    1 small onion, chopped
    ⅛ teaspoon pepper
    1 teaspoon monosodium glutamate
    ¼ cup flour
    ½ teaspoon salt
    ⅛ teaspoon pepper
    3 whole chicken breasts, split
    6-8 tablespoons butter or margarine

1. Combine first 10 ingredients in sauce pan; cover; cook over <u>low</u> heat 20 minutes.
2. Combine flour, salt, pepper; dust over both sides of chicken breasts.
3. Melt butter in 10-inch broiler pan; brown chicken on both sides—about 15 minutes.
4. Pour peach sauce over chicken; cover; reduce heat to <u>low</u>; cook 45-60 minutes or until chicken is fork tender.
5. Serve with sauce.
6. Six servings.

46

CHICKEN PIE

1 4-pound chicken
  Boiling water
1 tablespoon salt
2 stalks celery
1 bay leaf
1 medium onion, sliced
3 cups cooked diced potatoes
2 cups cooked diced carrots
1 cup cooked or canned peas
7 tablespoons butter or fat from chicken
7 tablespoons flour
1 teaspoon salt
⅛ teaspoon pepper
1 cup milk or cream
2 cups chicken broth
  Dash nutmeg
½ teaspoon Worcestershire sauce
  Pinch tarragon

1. Wash, clean chicken; cut into desired serving pieces.
2. Place in round roaster.
3. Add boiling water to cover chicken half way.
4. Add salt, celery, bay leaf, onion.
5. Cover; simmer until fork tender; allow 1-1½ hours for roaster; 3-4 hours for older fowl; additional water may be added if necessary.
6. Remove chicken; allow to cool.
7. Strain broth; add water to make 2 cups; skim off fat as it cools.
8. Remove skin from chicken; cut meat into 1-inch cubes.
9. Arrange chicken, potatoes, carrots, peas in casserole or shallow baking pan.
10. Melt fat in sauce pan; remove from heat.
11. Stir in flour, salt, pepper.
12. Add milk, chicken broth, nutmeg, Worcestershire sauce, tarragon.
13. Cook over low heat, stirring constantly until thickened.
14. Pour over chicken-vegetable mixture.
15. Top with baking powder biscuits or flaky pie crust.
16. Brush with milk.
17. Bake 20-25 minutes at 425°F.
18. Six servings.

VARIATIONS:
1. Leftover chicken may be used.
2. Part chicken, part ham may be used.
3. Heap fluffy mashed white or sweet potatoes on top instead of biscuits or pie crust.

GOLDEN CHICKEN '49

1 2-pound broiler or fryer, cut into serving pieces
¾ teaspoon salt
¼ cup butter or margarine
3 tablespoons flour
¼ cup sugar
¾ teaspoon salt
¼ teaspoon dry mustard
¼ teaspoon cinnamon
1½ cups orange juice
1 whole orange

1. Sprinkle chicken with salt.
2. Melt butter in 10-inch broiler pan; add chicken; brown on all sides; remove chicken.
3. Add flour, sugar, salt, dry mustard, cinnamon to drippings; stir to smooth paste.
4. Gradually add orange juice; cook, stirring constantly until mixture boils; add chicken; cover; simmer over low heat 35 minutes.
5. Grate 1 tablespoon orange rind; cut membrane from orange; cut out sections.
6. When chicken is tender, sprinkle orange rind and sections over chicken; cook 5 minutes longer.
7. Two servings.

CHICKEN LIVERS SAUTÉ

½ pound chicken livers
¼ cup butter or margarine
1 cup commercial sour cream
½ teaspoon salt
⅛ teaspoon pepper

1. Clean, cut livers into halves.
2. Sauté in butter in 10-inch broiler pan until lightly browned.
3. Add sour cream, salt, pepper; blend.
4. Serve over cooked rice or on toast.
5. Three-four servings.

VARIATION:
Mushrooms, a few slices green pepper or onion may be cooked with livers.

GIBLETS

1. Wash heart, liver, gizzard, neck.
2. Cook heart, gizzard, neck in water to cover; season with salt, pepper, a small bay leaf, a little diced onion, celery, carrot.
3. Simmer covered until gizzard is fork tender; add liver 10-20 minutes before giblets are done. Chicken giblets . . . 1-1½ hours; Turkey giblets . . . 2-3 hours.
4. Giblets may be diced and added to gravy or used in the stuffing. Use broth in making gravy.

ROAST TURKEY

1. Wash; clean; dry turkey. Rub inside with salt, about ⅛ teaspoon per pound.
2. Fill cavity, neck opening with desired stuffing; pack lightly as stuffing swells during cooking. Turkey may also be roasted unstuffed.
3. Close cavity with skewers; lace with cord. Pull neck skin back over stuffing; fasten with skewers.
4. Using long cord, tie ends of legs together; bring cord from legs down around tail, drawing it just tight enough to hold legs down, yet not too close to body. When bird is two thirds done, cut cord around legs.
5. Bend tip ends of wings backward so they are held against back of bird.
6. Grease turkey thoroughly with soft butter; sprinkle with salt, pepper.
7. Line shallow open roasting pan with Alcoa Wrap.
8. Place bird, breast side up on rack in pan. If using a V-type rack, place breast down, turning bird when about half done.
9. Fold piece of Alcoa Wrap, 4-5 inches longer than bird, in half lengthwise to form a tent.
10. Place tent over turkey, pressing one end lightly around drumsticks, other around neck opening.
11. Add no water; occasional basting with drippings in pan improves flavor.
12. If wrapper has a printed time-temperature chart, use those directions. Otherwise, use following chart as a guide.

CHART FOR ROAST TURKEY

Time Guide
Oven Temperature 325°F.

Purchased Weight	Approximate Total Time * Stuffed	Approximate Total Time ** Unstuffed
8-10 lbs.	3½-4¼ hrs.	3 — 3½ hrs.
10-12 lbs.	4¼-4¾ hrs.	3½-4 hrs.
12-14 lbs.	4¾-5½ hrs.	4 — 4½ hrs.
14-16 lbs.	5½-6 hrs.	4½-5 hrs.
16-18 lbs.	6 — 6¾ hrs.	5 — 5½ hrs.
18-20 lbs.	6¾-7½ hrs.	5½-6 hrs.
20-24 lbs.	7½-8¾ hrs.	6 — 7 hrs.

* Five minutes per pound has been added for stuffed bird.

** Total time has been based on oven-ready weight of turkey which is purchased weight of turkey minus neck and giblets packed inside bird. The oven-ready weight is from 1 to 3 pounds less than the purchased weight, depending on size of bird.

When using the Time-Temperature Chart, keep in mind that meat and bone structure of turkeys vary greatly because of new raising and feeding methods. For this reason, times given are approximate, and should serve only as a guide.

Start to test for doneness about one-half hour before bird is supposed to be done. Fowl is done when leg will move up and down freely. Another test is to press the thickest part of the drumstick between the fingers—meat should be soft. Protect fingers with piece of paper towel.

Turkey will be juicier and easier to carve if allowed to set 15-20 minutes before carving. Any left-over meat and stuffing should be removed from the carcass, wrapped separately and stored in the refrigerator for later use.

CHICKEN OR TURKEY DEVONSHIRE

1. Heat 1 can cream of mushroom soup; thin with ½ cup cream; add 1 cup grated Cheddar cheese; stir until cheese is melted.
2. Arrange sliced white meat of turkey or chicken on white toast; top with slice of baked ham, mushroom sauce.
3. Place under broiler until sauce bubbles and browns slightly.

MAGGIE'S CHICKEN MORNAY

Part One
    4 breasts of chicken
    ½ cup flour
    1 teaspoon salt
    ⅛ teaspoon pepper
    ⅛ teaspoon ginger
    ½ cup butter or margarine
    1 cup water

Part Two
    4 tablespoons butter or margarine
    4 tablespoons flour
    1 teaspoon salt
    ½ cup cream
    ½ cup milk
    1 cup liquid from fry pan
    1 cup grated American cheese
    1 cup diced canned mushrooms

Part One
1. Coat chicken breasts with flour combined with salt, pepper, ginger.
2. Brown on all sides in butter in 10-inch broiler pan over <u>medium</u> heat.
3. Cover; cook over <u>low</u> heat 30-45 minutes or until fork tender; a little water may be added if necessary.
4. Place breasts in shallow baking pan.
5. Add water to drippings in fry pan; stir to loosen any sediment in pan.

Part Two
1. Melt butter in sauce pan; remove from heat.
2. Add flour, salt; blend thoroughly.
3. Add cream; blend.
4. Add milk, liquid from broiler pan.
5. Return to <u>low</u> heat; cook, stirring constantly until thickened.
6. Add ½ cup cheese; stir until melted.
7. Add mushrooms.
8. Pour sauce over chicken.
9. Sprinkle remaining grated cheese over top.
10. Bake 25-30 minutes at 350°F. until cheese is melted, just lightly browned.
11. Sprinkle with paprika; serve at once.
12. Four servings.

ROAST DUCK

Select 3½-4½ pound duck drawn weight.

1. Clean; wash; dry duck.
2. Fill cavity with quartered apples, two large quartered onions, several stalks of celery to give flavor but remove before serving.
3. Truss bird or not as needed; sometimes legs and wings are too short to truss. Sprinkle with salt, pepper.
4. Place duck breast side up in V rack in utility pan.
5. Do not grease; add no water; do not cover. Do not prick skin with fork as this allows juices to escape.
6. Roast 40-45 minutes per pound at 325°F. Roasting time may vary. Duck is done when drumstick will move up and down freely.
7. Five minutes before duck is done pour Orange Sauce, page 65, over duck.
8. Four servings.

LEFTOVER DAYS

Leftover chicken or turkey is good in a salad or as a sandwich filling.
Invite the girls for lunch and serve this special sandwich of ours. For each sandwich place one slice rye bread on a dinner plate; spread with butter. Place lettuce leaf on bread; top with a slice of Swiss cheese. Add another lettuce leaf; cover with one or two slices of leftover chicken or turkey. Pour about ½ cup Thousand Island Dressing over sandwich. Top with a tomato slice and a slice of hard cooked egg. Cross two slices of crisply cooked bacon on top. Garnish with a ripe olive, sprig of parsley.
Combine in a casserole one can cream of chicken soup, undiluted, with diced leftover chicken or turkey, leftover peas and carrots. Top with buttered soft bread crumbs. Bake 20–25 minutes at 350°F. or until lightly browned and bubbly.
Of course, there is always creamed or a la king chicken or turkey to use up the last little pieces.

WILD RICE STUFFING

  ¾ cup wild rice, washed
2½ cups boiling water
  2 tablespoons butter or margarine
  2 tablespoons chopped celery
  1 tablespoon chopped onion
  1 tablespoon chopped green pepper
  ½ teaspoon sage
    Salt, pepper

1. Cook wild rice in boiling water 15 minutes; drain.
2. Melt butter in 10-inch broiler pan; add celery, onion, green pepper, sage, salt, pepper; cook over <u>low</u> heat 5 minutes.
3. Add wild rice; blend.
4. Sufficient stuffing for 2 Cornish hens or 1 pheasant.

CHESTNUT STUFFING

  ½ pound chestnuts
  1 tablespoon butter or margarine
  ½ pound sausage meat
  ¼ cup minced onion
  ½ cup hot water
  1 teaspoon dried sage
1½ teaspoons salt
  ⅛ teaspoon pepper
  4 cups cubed bread

1. Wash chestnuts; make a long slit through shell on both sides of chestnut; bake in very hot (500°F.) oven 15 minutes. Remove from oven; remove shells, skin. Boil chestnuts in salted water to cover 20 minutes; drain; chop fine.
2. Melt butter in 10-inch broiler pan; sauté sausage, onion until sausage is thoroughly cooked.
3. Add water, sage, salt, pepper, bread crumbs, chestnuts; toss lightly.
4. Sufficient stuffing for 4 pound fowl.

BREAD STUFFING

  6 tablespoons butter or margarine
  ½ cup chopped celery
  2 tablespoons minced onion
  2 tablespoons chopped parsley
  4 cups cubed bread
    (approximately 12 slices)
  ½ teaspoon sage or poultry
    seasoning
  1 teaspoon salt
  ¼ teaspoon pepper

1. Melt butter in 10-inch broiler pan; add chopped celery, onion, parsley. Cook together three minutes; add bread, seasonings; toss.
2. Stuff chicken. The neck pocket will hold about ¾ cup stuffing; the body the rest.
3. Sufficient stuffing for 4 pound chicken.
NOTE: Three times the recipe sufficient for 12 pound turkey.

OYSTER STUFFING

  1 cup stewing oysters, chopped
  4 cups stale bread cubes
  2 teaspoons salt
  ⅛ teaspoon pepper
  ⅛ teaspoon sage
  3 tablespoons butter or margarine
  1 onion, minced
  2 tablespoons finely chopped parsley
  ¾ cup finely chopped celery

1. Chop oysters coarsely; put into sauce pan; cover; cook over <u>medium</u> heat 5 minutes; reduce heat to <u>low</u>. Cook 4-5 minutes or until edges of oysters curl.
2. Drain well; save liquor if desired, for use in gravy.
3. Place bread cubes in bowl; add salt, pepper, sage; toss lightly to mix.
4. In 10-inch broiler pan, place butter, onion, parsley, celery; cover; cook over <u>medium</u> heat 5 minutes; reduce heat to <u>low</u>; cook 5-7 minutes or until onion is clear. Remove cover; brown lightly.
5. Pour over seasoned bread cubes; toss together to mix well; add oysters; mix.
6. Sufficient stuffing for 4 pound fowl.

FISH

BROILED FISH

1. Scale; split; clean fish; wipe dry.
2. Melt 2 tablespoons shortening in 10-inch broiler pan over medium heat.
3. Place fish in pan; skin side up.
4. Reduce heat to medium-low.
5. Broil 15-20 minutes or until golden brown and tender.
6. This method is used for all small fish such as bass, pickerel, blue fish, red snapper, white fish, trout and mackerel.

SALTED FISH

1. Place fish flesh side down in pan.
2. Cover with cold water; soak 48 hours.
3. Drain; add fresh water to cover.
4. Cover; bring to boil; simmer 20 minutes or until tender.
5. Drain; serve with Tomato Sauce.

TO POACH FISH

1. Put 2 cups boiling water into 10-inch broiler pan; add 1½ teaspoons salt, 1 slice lemon, 1 slice onion, 2 sprigs parsley, ¼ teaspoon pepper, 1 bay leaf; boil 5 minutes.
2. Reduce heat to low; add fish; cover; simmer gently 10 minutes or until fish flakes easily with a fork. If fish is thick, turn once during cooking.

TO COOK FRESH SHRIMP

1. Place 1 quart water, a slice of lemon in bottom of round roaster. Adjust steamer plate; cover. Place over high heat until water comes to rapid boil.
2. Wash shrimp in cold water; place on steamer plate; cover. Reduce heat to medium; steam 15 minutes.
3. Remove shells. With paring knife cut around circumference deep enough to expose black thread which is the intestine. Remove all of intestine.

STEAMED FISH

1. Sprinkle fish with salt; place on No. 817 steamer plate.
2. Steam covered over boiling water until tender or until meat can be readily flaked with a fork.
3. Fish with a dry meat such as cod, haddock, halibut, salmon are best for steaming.
4. Steamed fish may be served hot with sauce or chilled and flaked for use in salads.

SOUTHERN STYLE PERCH

  12 fillets of perch
   2 eggs, well beaten
   3 tablespoons flour
   5 tablespoons shortening
      Salt, pepper, paprika
  ½ cup tomato paste
  ½ cup milk
   1 teaspoon cornstarch

1. Dip fish into egg; roll in flour.
2. Melt sortening in 10-inch broiler pan over medium heat.
3. Brown six fillets at a time.
4. After all are browned, place together; season wtih salt, pepper, paprika.
5. Reduce heat to low; cover; cook 20 minutes.
6. Remove fillets to platter.
7. Combine tomato paste, milk, cornstarch; add to drippings in pan.
8. Bring to boil; pour over fish.
9. Six servings.
NOTE: All skinless fillets may be prepared this way. Serve plain or with sauce.

SHRIMP FLOUNDER ROLLS

6 flounder fillets
Salt, pepper
1 tablespoon mayonnaise
1 teaspoon prepared mustard
2 tablespoons softened butter or
    margarine
2 tablespoons minced parsley
1 pound shrimp, cooked, shelled,
    cleaned
2 tablespoons shortening
2 cups canned tomatoes
⅔ cup soft bread crumbs
6 tablespoons butter or margarine,
    melted

1. Cut each fillet in half lengthwise; rub with salt, pepper.
2. Blend together mayonnaise, mustard, butter, parsley; spread mixture over fillets.
3. Place 2 shrimp in each fillet; roll like jelly roll with shrimp inside; fasten with toothpicks.
4. Melt shortening in 10-inch broiler pan over <u>medium</u> heat; add rolls, remaining shrimp.
5. Pour tomatoes over all.
6. Brown bread crumbs in melted butter; sprinkle over top; cover.
7. Reduce heat to <u>low</u>; cook 25 minutes.
8. Six servings.

CREOLE SHRIMP

4 tablespoons butter or margarine
2 green onions, chopped
½ green pepper, chopped
1 cup celery, chopped
¼ teaspoon crushed sage
1 teaspoon salt
¼ teaspoon Tobasco sauce
1 cup tomato juice
2 cups cleaned raw shrimp
2 cups cooked rice

1. Melt butter in 10-inch broiler pan; brown onion, pepper, celery lightly.
2. Add sage, salt, Tabasco sauce, tomato juice; bring to boil.
3. Add shrimp; simmer uncovered 30 minutes.
4. Serve over rice.
5. Four servings.

OYSTERS KILPATRICK

1 dozen large oysters or 1 12-ounce
    can frozen oysters, thawed
1½ teaspoons lemon juice
    Dash pepper
¼ cup tomato paste
½ cup grated sharp cheese
1 strip bacon, cut into 6 pieces
    Dash paprika

1. Cut out 6 circles from double-thick squares of Alcoa Wrap using saucer for pattern; turn up edges ½-inch around circles to form casseroles.
2. Wash, drain oysters; place in foil casseroles.
3. Sprinkle ¼ teaspoon lemon juice, dash pepper over each casserole.
4. Spread tomato paste on oysters; cover with 1 tablespoon grated cheese; lay piece of bacon on cheese; place 1 more teaspoon grated cheese on bacon; top with dash of paprika.
5. Place casseroles on baking sheet; bake 10 minutes at 500°F.
6. Six servings.

FISH ON-A-SILVER SEA

1 2½-pound whole fish
1½ cups soft bread cubes
½ teaspoon salt
1 small onion, minced
¼ cup celery, chopped
1 tablespoon lemon juice
⅓ cup melted butter or margarine
1 tablespoon parsley, cut fine

1. Clean fish; bone; remove head, tail.
2. Dry; sprinkle inside with salt.
3. Combine bread cubes, salt, onion, celery, lemon juice; pack lightly into fish.
4. Secure opening with skewers; rub outside of fish with butter.
5. Line shallow baking pan with sheet of ALCOA WRAP; place fish in foil-lined pan.
6. Bake 1 hour at 375°F.
7. Pick up edges of foil; remove fish on foil to serving platter; push foil down around fish to make silver sea.
8. Serve with lemon butter.
9. Six servings.

SEAFOOD NEWBURG

      6 tablespoons butter or margarine
      2 tablespoons flour
  1⅓ cups milk
  ⅔ cup light cream
      3 egg yolks, slightly beaten
      1 teaspoon salt
  ⅛ teaspoon nutmeg
      Dash paprika
      2 6½-ounce cans shrimp, lobster
          or crab meat
  ¼ cup Sherry wine
      Toast points

1. Melt butter in 10-inch broiler pan.
2. Stir in flour; gradually add milk, cream, stirring constantly.
3. Cook over <u>low</u> heat until slightly thickened.
4. Slowly stir in egg yolks; continue cooking until thickened, stirring constantly.
5. Add salt, nutmeg, paprika, seafood; continue cooking until seafood is hot.
6. Just before serving, stir in Sherry.
7. Serve over toast points.
8. Six servings.

FISH BAKE SUPREME

      6 ounces thin spaghetti, uncooked
  ½ cup butter or margarine, melted
  ¼ cup chopped parsley
      1 tablespoon lemon juice
      1 teaspoon grated onion
  ⅓ cup chutney, cut fine
  ½ teaspoon salt
  ¼ teaspoon pepper
  ¾ pound frozen fish fillets, thawed

1. Cook spaghetti in boiling salted water until tender; drain.
2. Combine butter, parsley, lemon juice, onion, chutney, salt, pepper.
3. Add about two-thirds butter mixture to spaghetti.
4. Pour mixture into lightly greased 1½-quart casserole.
5. Arrange fish fillets on top.
6. Pour remaining butter mixture over fish.
7. Cover casserole with foil; bake 30 minutes at 350°F.; remove cover; bake about 5 minutes longer.
8. Four servings.

SOUTHERN CRAB CAKES

      2 6½-ounce cans crab meat, drained,
          boned, flaked
      1 teaspoon salt
  ¾ teaspoon dry mustard
  ¼ teaspoon pepper
      2 eggs, slightly beaten
  1½ teaspoons Worcestershire sauce
      2 teaspoons mayonnaise
  ¼ cup butter or margarine, melted
  1½ teaspoons snipped parsley
      1 cup dry bread crumbs
      1 egg, slightly beaten
      2 tablespoons water
  ½ cup dry bread crumbs
  4-6 tablespoons butter or margarine

1. Mix crab meat, salt, mustard, pepper, eggs, Worcestershire sauce, mayonnaise, melted butter, parsley, bread crumbs; toss together lightly; chill 1 hour.
2. Shape into 6 medium-sized flat patties.
3. Dip patties into egg and water which have been mixed together, then into remaining ½ cup bread crumbs.
4. Melt remaining butter in 10-inch broiler pan; add cakes; fry until golden brown on both sides—about 15 minutes—adding more butter if necessary.
5. Serve with Tartar Sauce.
6. Six servings.

OYSTER STEW

1. Melt ¼ cup butter or margarine in 10-inch broiler pan; add ¼ teaspoon grated onion, 24 drained oysters; heat only until edges of oysters curl slightly.
2. Add 1 pint milk, 1 pint cream, ¾ teaspoon salt, ⅛ teaspoon pepper; heat over <u>medium-low</u> heat but do not boil.
3. Serve with dash of paprika, lump of butter.
4. Four servings.

Dried Foods

WHEN the budget needs stretching or you feel adventuresome, try including some of today's new improved dried foods in your menus.

Fruits and vegetables no longer need overnight soaking. They cook to plumpy tenderness in no time at all. Cereals and now even some varieties of macaroni, spaghetti and noodles have been given the magic touch that makes them ready to serve in a matter of minutes.

HOW TO COOK DRIED FRUITS AND VEGETABLES

1. When doing a low roast, dried fruits and vegetables may be cooked in the No. 802 pan on the steamer plate or set into the No. 807 steamer ring directly over the meat after it has been browned.

2. Use one cup of water to two cups fruit or vegetables. Sugar may be added to fruits near end of cooking time. For a vegetable, add ½ teaspoon salt for each cup of water at start of cooking.

3. Cook fruits 30-45 minutes or until plump and tender. Cook vegetables 1-2 hours. To test for doneness, remove a few with a spoon. If skins burst when you blow on them and they are soft, the vegetable is done.

ALTERNATE METHOD: Dried fruits and vegetables may be cooked by bringing one quart of water to a boil in the round roaster and placing No. 802 inner pan containing water, vegetable or fruit in the No. 807 steamer ring. Add cover; reduce heat to low. Cooking times will be the same as given above.

CEREALS: Today especially, breakfast cereals such as oatmeal, fine grain wheat cereals and cornmeal are of the quick-cook variety. They are best prepared in a sauce pan according to directions on the package.

Rice, also classed as a cereal, is either of the precooked or regular variety. Precooked rice should be cooked according to directions on package.

To cook regular rice: Bring 2½ cups water to a boil in sauce pan. Add 1 cup rice, 1 teaspoon salt. Cover; cook over <u>low</u> heat about 25 minutes or until all water has been absorbed. Rinsing or draining is not necessary. Each grain of rice will be tender and dry. One cup raw rice makes four cups cooked rice.

MACARONI, SPAGHETTI AND NOODLES are of either the precooked or regular variety. Most of the precooked pastas—macaroni, spaghetti, noodles—need only be rehydrated and heated. They should be prepared according to directions on the package.

Regular macaroni, spaghetti and noodles are best cooked in boiling salted water until tender, then rinsed and drained. A sauce pan or the broiler pan may be used for small quantities, the round roaster for larger amounts.

SERVING SUGGESTIONS

FLUFFY RICE is a welcome change from potatoes especially with ham or chicken. For family cheers, top with creamy gravy.

Serve with Beef Stroganoff, page 34, Chicken Livers, page 47 or Lamb Curry, page 39.

Pack cooked rice in a buttered 1½ quart ring mold, then set in pan of hot water and simmer 10 minutes. Unmold on hot platter and fill center with creamed chicken or turkey or lamb curry.

Make a Rice Loaf by combining 2½ cups cooked rice with 1 cup Thin Cream Sauce, page 64, 1 egg yolk, 1 cup canned salmon or tuna fish, ¼ cup bread crumbs, ½ cup chopped celery, 1 tablespoon each chopped onion and parsley, 1 teaspoon lemon juice and a dash of salt, pepper and paprika. Pack into No. 802 inner pan and steam over boiling water about 30 minutes. Good with tomato sauce.

Add a chicken bouillon cube to the water when cooking rice. Rub broiler pan with the cut side of a clove of garlic; add 1–2 tablespoons butter. Allow to melt over <u>low</u> heat, then add rice, a few cooked fine noodles and some pignolia nuts. Cook, stirring until well blended. Wonderful with broiled lamb chops.

Left over rice may be added to tomato or chicken soup, used in many casserole dishes, with chopped meat in stuffed peppers or added to a chicken or seafood salad.

DRIED FRUITS are excellent substitutes for fresh fruits.

Cook peaches, apricots, prunes and pears together for a fruit compote to serve at breakfast or as a relish with the meat, fowl or fish at dinner.

Cooked apricots put through the food press make a delicious sauce for cake squares, ice cream or cup custard.

Prunes served with a dash of lemon juice go well with hot buttered toast for breakfast.

MACARONI, NOODLES AND SPAGHETTI, like rice are also a good substitute for potatoes. Macaroni added to Cheese Sauce, page 64, makes everyone's favorite macaroni and cheese.

For a one dish meal, add cooked shrimp to macaroni and cheese, top with sliced tomatoes seasoned with basil and bake 25–30 minutes at 350°F.

Cooked shell or bow knot macaroni tossed with melted butter and grated Parmesan cheese is a new taste treat.

Combine cooked macaroni with seasoned beaten eggs. Pour into melted butter in broiler pan; cook over <u>low</u> heat stirring constantly until eggs are set. Top with chopped parsley.

Substitute cooked elbow macaroni for the potatoes in your favorite potato salad recipe. You will like the results.

Broad or medium noodles may be used in place of macaroni in any of the above suggestions except for the salad.

Noodles, cooked and tossed with melted butter, go well with any meat. Left-over noodles may be added to soup or used in casserole dishes.

Spaghetti, of course, is at its best topped with sauce. Use our recipe for Spaghetti Sauce, page 66, or one of the many canned spaghetti sauces on the market.

Glorious

Casseroles

Everybody loves casserole dishes. A good cook learns early in her career that a casserole dish creates the perfect disguise for leftovers, comes to her rescue when the budget needs stretching and can solve many an entertaining problem. Pretty as a picture and smelling divine, it comes right to the table to be served piping hot. And there's no "after scouring" if you line your casserole with Alcoa Wrap.

Recipes

TAMALE RICE WITH FRANKFURTERS

    2 tablespoons shortening
    1 onion, chopped
    2 tablespoons vinegar
    2 tablespoons brown sugar
    1 tablespoon lemon juice
    1 cup ketchup
    1 cup stock or water
    2 teaspoons salt
    1 tablespoon Worcestershire sauce
    3 cups cooked rice
    6 frankfurters

1. Melt shortening in 10-inch broiler pan; add onion; brown.
2. Add vinegar, brown sugar, lemon juice, ketchup, stock, salt, Worcestershire sauce; cover; simmer 15 minutes.
3. Add cooked rice; pour into greased 2-quart casserole.
4. Arrange frankfurters on top.
5. Bake uncovered 35-40 minutes at 350°F.
6. Six servings.

BAKED BEANS

    1 pound dried lima beans
    1 quart cold water
    1 small onion, sliced
 1½ teaspoons salt
    2 teaspoons vinegar
    ½ teaspoon prepared mustard
    1 tablespoon brown sugar
    2 tablespoons ketchup
      Dash pepper
    ½ pound salt pork, diced

1. Combine beans, water in round roaster; cover; bring to boil; cook over low heat 30 minutes.
2. Mix together remaining ingredients; add to beans; stir until well blended. Pour into large casserole or bean pot.
3. Bake covered 4-5 hours at 275°F.; uncover last hour of baking. Add a little more water if necessary during baking.
4. Beans are done when soft and most of liquid is absorbed.
5. Six servings.

NOODLE PUDDING

- ¾ cup wide noodles, uncooked, coarsely broken
- 2 egg yolks
- 6 tablespoons sugar
- ¼ pound farmer's cheese (or dry cottage cheese)
- ½ cup commercial sour cream
- ¼ teaspoon salt
- 2 tablespoons raisins
- ½ teaspoon vanilla
- 2 egg whites beaten stiff

1. Cook noodles; drain; do not rinse.
2. Combine egg yolks, sugar; blend.
3. Add cheese, sour cream, salt, raisins, vanilla, noodles; blend well.
4. Beat egg whites until stiff but not dry; fold into noodle mixture.
5. Pour noodle mixture into lightly greased 1½-quart casserole; spread evenly.
6. Bake uncovered 50-60 minutes at 350°F. or until knife comes out clean.
7. Four servings.

SALMON CASSEROLE WITH LEMON CUCUMBER SAUCE

- 1½ cups water
- 1½ cups packaged pre-cooked rice
- 2 tablespoons instant minced onion
- ¼ cup cold water
- 1 pound can salmon, drained, flaked
- 2 teaspoons salt
- ¼ teaspoon pepper
- 2 egg whites
- 1 egg, whole
- 2 tablespoons butter or margarine, melted

1. Bring water to boil in sauce pan; add rice; cover; remove from heat; let stand 5 minutes.
2. Combine onion, cold water; let stand 5 minutes.
3. Combine rice, onion, salmon, salt, pepper.
4. Beat egg whites, egg; add to salmon mixture; blend well.
5. Press into 1½-quart casserole; brush top with melted butter.
6. Bake uncovered 30 minutes at 375°F.
7. Garnish with lemon wedges, parsley; serve with Lemon Cucumber Sauce, page 65.
8. Four-five servings.

CHICKEN DIVAN

- 2 pounds asparagus
- 1 10½-ounce can condensed cream of chicken soup, undiluted
- ¼ teaspoon nutmeg
- 1 teaspoon Worcestershire sauce
- 1 cup grated Parmesan cheese
- 1 cup sliced cooked chicken or turkey
- ½ cup heavy cream, whipped
- ¾ cup mayonnaise or Hollandaise sauce

1. Prepare, cook asparagus.
2. Place in 2-quart casserole.
3. Combine soup, nutmeg, Worcestershire sauce; pour half of mixture over asparagus; sprinkle with ⅓ cup of the cheese.
4. Top with chicken; pour over remaining soup mixture; sprinkle with ⅓ cup cheese.
5. Bake uncovered 25 minutes at 400°F.
6. Fold whipped cream into mayonnaise or Hollandaise sauce; spread over chicken; sprinkle with ⅓ cup of the cheese.
7. Broil 2-3 minutes or until golden brown.
8. Six servings.

DEVILED MUSHROOMS

- 3 cups fresh mushrooms
- Salt, pepper
- 1 tablespoon lemon juice
- 2 hard-cooked egg yolks
- 2 raw egg yolks, beaten
- 1 cup soft bread crumbs
- 2 tablespoons butter, softened
- Dash of Tabasco sauce

1. Wash mushrooms; drain; dry; remove stems.
2. Place mushroom caps, stems in lightly greased 2½-quart casserole.
3. Season with salt, pepper, lemon juice.
4. Mash hard-cooked egg yolks; add raw egg yolks, bread crumbs, butter, Tabasco sauce; blend well.
5. Sprinkle egg-bread crumb mixture on top of mushrooms.
6. Bake 25-30 minutes at 350°F.
7. Six servings.

PERFECT CASSEROLE

    1 pound ground beef
 ¼ cup commercial sour cream
 1½ tablespoons dried onion soup
      (mix well before measuring)
    1 egg, slightly beaten
 ¾ cup soft bread crumbs
    3 tablespoons flour
 ½ teaspoon paprika
    2 tablespoons butter or margarine
 ½ cup canned sliced mushrooms with
      liquid
 ¾ cup condensed cream of chicken soup
 ¾ cup water

1. Mix meat, cream, onion soup, egg, bread crumbs together; shape into 8 balls.
2. Roll meat balls in flour blended with paprika.
3. Melt butter in 10-inch broiler pan; brown meat balls on all sides.
4. Combine mushrooms with liquid, cream of chicken soup, water; pour over balls.
5. Cover; simmer over low heat 20 minutes.
6. Pour into 1½-quart casserole.
7. Top with Butter Crumb Dumplings, page 82.
8. Bake uncovered 20-25 minutes at 400F°.
9. Four servings.

VEAL CASSEROLE WITH CURRY BISCUITS

 ¼ cup butter or margarine
 ¼ cup chopped onion
 ¼ cup minced green pepper
 ¼ cup flour
    2 chicken bouillon cubes
    2 cups hot water
    3 cups cubed cooked veal
 ¼ cup chopped pimiento

1. Melt butter in 10-inch broiler pan.
2. Add onion, green pepper; cook until tender.
3. Blend in flour; add chicken bouillon cubes dissolved in water; cook until thickened.
4. Add veal, pimiento; mix thoroughly.
5. Place in 2-quart casserole; bake uncovered 10 minutes at 425°F.
6. Remove from oven; top with Curry Biscuits, page 81; bake 10 minutes longer.
7. Six servings.

SHRIMP CASSEROLE HARPIN

    2 pounds large fresh shrimp
    1 tablespoon lemon juice
    3 tablespoons salad oil
 ¾ cup raw regular or processed rice
    2 tablespoons butter or margarine
 ¼ cup minced green pepper
 ¼ cup minced onion
    1 teaspoon salt
 ⅛ teaspoon pepper
 ⅛ teaspoon mace
      Dash cayenne pepper
    1 can condensed tomato soup, undiluted
    1 cup heavy cream
 ½ cup slivered almonds
 ½ cup Sherry wine
      Paprika

1. Shell, clean, cook shrimp in boiling salted water 5 minutes; drain.
2. Place in 2-quart casserole; sprinkle with lemon juice, oil.
3. Cook rice as package directs; drain.
4. Melt butter in 10-inch broiler pan; add green pepper, onion; sauté 5 minutes; add rice, salt, pepper, mace, cayenne pepper, tomato soup, cream, ¼ cup of the slivered almonds, Sherry wine; pour over shrimp.
5. Top with remaining almonds; sprinkle with paprika.
6. Bake uncovered approximately 55 minutes at 350°F. or until bubbly.
7. Six servings.

MACARONI, HAM AND CHEESE

    3 tablespoons butter or margarine
 ¼ cup flour
    2 cups hot milk
    1 teaspoon salt
 ⅛ teaspoon cayenne pepper
    2 cups cooked macaroni
 ¾ pound cooked ham, cut into cubes
 ½ pound sharp cheese, grated

1. Melt butter in sauce pan; add flour; stir until smooth; add hot milk, stirring constantly; cook over medium-low heat until thickened, smooth.
2. Add salt, pepper; pour cream sauce over macaroni.
3. Put alternate layers of creamed macaroni, ham, cheese in greased 2-quart casserole; sprinkle cheese over top.
4. Bake uncovered 30 minutes at 350°F.
5. Six servings.

Recipes for Eggs Plain and Fancy

FRIED EGGS

1. Melt butter or margarine in 10-inch broiler pan or fry pan over <u>medium</u> heat until bubbly; reduce heat to <u>simmer</u>.
2. Break eggs into bowl; pour into pan.
3. Sprinkle with salt, pepper; cover; <u>turn off heat</u>. There will be sufficient heat in the pan to complete the cooking.
4. Allow eggs to cook <u>just until</u> white is set. There should be no browning, crusty edges or sticking.

SCRAMBLED EGGS

    2 tablespoons butter or margarine
    8 eggs
    ¾ teaspoon salt
    ⅛ teaspoon pepper
    ¾ cup milk

1. Melt butter in 10-inch broiler pan over <u>low</u> heat.
2. Beat eggs slightly; add remaining ingredients; beat thoroughly.
3. Pour into pan; cook over <u>low</u> heat, stirring constantly.
4. Four servings.

FRENCH OMELET

    2 tablespoons butter or margarine, melted
    8 eggs
    1 tablespoon cold water
    1 teaspoon salt
    Dash pepper

1. Line 10-inch broiler pan with heavy duty Alcoa Wrap, extending foil up sides of pan, allowing enough to grasp easily.
2. Brush foil generously with melted butter.
3. Place broiler pan over <u>low</u> heat.
4. Combine eggs, water, salt, pepper; beat until just blended.
5. Pour eggs into pre-heated foil lined broiler pan.
6. As mixture starts to set at edge, lift this portion gently with spatula and move the foil so that uncooked portions flow to bottom.
7. When eggs are set and surface is still moist, increase heat to brown bottom quickly.
8. Lift omelet from broiler pan with extended foil; fold one side over the other; flip onto platter.
9. Four servings.

SCRAMBLED EGGS DE LUXE

>3 tablespoons butter or margarine
>8 eggs
>½ cup milk
>Salt, pepper to taste
>4 slices Swiss cheese
>1 tablespoon fine bread crumbs

1. Melt 2 tablespoons of the butter in 10-inch broiler pan.
2. Beat eggs with milk, salt, pepper.
3. Pour into broiler pan; cook over <u>low</u> heat, stirring constantly, until eggs are set but still soft.
4. Top with cheese slices; dot with remaining butter, crumbs; cover.
5. Continue cooking over <u>low</u> heat 10 minutes.
6. Four servings.

PUFFY OMELET

>4 eggs, separated
>4 tablespoons hot water
>¾ teaspoons salt
>⅛ teaspoon pepper
>1 tablespoon butter or margarine, melted

1. Beat egg whites until stiff; set aside. Beat yolks until thick and lemon colored; beat in hot water; add salt, pepper.
2. Fold egg whites into yolks.
3. Butter bottom, sides of 10-inch broiler pan; heat over <u>low</u> heat 5 minutes.
4. Pour egg mixture into pan; cook uncovered until top is firm to the touch.
5. Fold in half; turn onto platter; serve at once.
6. If desired, ¾ cup diced cooked meat, ⅓ cup grated American cheese, 1 cup cooked vegetable or ½ cup tomato sauce may be spread over top before folding.
7. Two servings.

SAVORY SCRAMBLED EGGS

>¼ cup butter or margarine
>12 eggs, beaten
>⅔ cup milk
>Salt, pepper
>2 3-ounce packages cream cheese, cut in ½-inch squares

1. Melt butter in 10-inch broiler pan.
2. Combine eggs, milk, seasonings; pour into pan.
3. Cook over <u>low</u> heat, stirring constantly until eggs begin to thicken.
4. Add cream cheese cut in squares.
5. Continue cooking, stirring until cheese is blended and eggs are firm but moist.
6. Six servings.

BENEDICT-STYLE EGGS

>2 tablespoons butter or margarine
>½ cup minced onions
>1 10-ounce can condensed cream of mushroom soup, undiluted
>⅓ cup milk
>6 eggs
>3 English muffins, split
>6 thin slices cooked ham

1. Melt butter in 10-inch broiler pan; saute onions until tender.
2. Blend in soup, milk; heat to boiling.
3. Reduce heat to <u>low</u>; break eggs into sauce; cook covered about 10 minutes, or until eggs are of desired doneness.
4. Split muffins; toast under broiler; butter.
5. Top toasted muffin half with ham slice, then egg.
6. Six servings.

Sauce Sorcery

SAUCES FOR VEGETABLES

WHITE OR CREAM SAUCES

Thin White or Cream Sauce
    1 tablespoon butter or margarine
    1 tablespoon flour
    ¼ teaspoon salt
    1 cup milk

Medium White or Cream Sauce
    2 tablespoons butter or margarine
    2 tablespoons flour
    ¼ teaspoon salt
    1 cup milk

Thick White or Cream Sauce
    3 tablespoons butter or margarine
    3 tablespoons flour
    ¼ teaspoon salt
    1 cup milk

1. Melt butter in sauce pan; remove from heat.
2. Add flour, salt; stir; add milk.
3. Cook over <u>low</u> heat, stirring constantly until thickened.
4. About 1 cup.

HOLLANDAISE SAUCE

    2 egg yolks
    ½ teaspoon salt
    Dash cayenne pepper
    ½ cup melted butter or margarine
    1 tablespoon lemon juice

1. Beat egg yolks until thick; add salt, pepper.
2. Add 3 tablespoons melted butter, a little at a time, beating constantly.
3. Slowly beat in remaining butter alternately with lemon juice.
4. Serve with green vegetables, especially broccoli or asparagus.
5. About ½ cup.

CHEESE SAUCE

    1 bouillon cube
    ½ cup boiling water
    2 tablespoons butter or margarine
    2 tablespoons flour
    ½ cup milk
    ½ teaspoon dry mustard
    ½ teaspoon Worcestershire sauce
    ¼ pound (1 cup) grated
    American cheese

1. Dissolve bouillon cube in boiling water.
2. Melt butter in sauce pan over <u>very</u> <u>low</u> heat; add flour; stir until smooth.
3. Gradually add milk, bouillon; cook, stirring constantly until smooth, thick.
4. Add mustard, Worcestershire sauce, cheese; stir until cheese is melted.
5. About 2 cups.
VARIATION:
For Quick Cheese Sauce, add 1 cup grated American Cheese to 1 cup Medium White or Cream Sauce.

SAUCES FOR MEATS

ORANGE SAUCE FOR DUCK

    1/3 cup brown sugar, firmly packed
    1/3 cup white sugar
    1 tablespoon cornstarch
    1/4 teaspoon salt
    1 tablespoon grated orange rind
    1 cup orange juice

1. Combine sugars, cornstarch, salt, orange rind in sauce pan.
2. Add enough juice to make paste, then stir in remaining juice.
3. Cook until clear, slightly thickened—about 3 minutes.
4. Serve with Roast Duck.
5. About 1¼ cups.

LEMON CUCUMBER SAUCE

    2 egg yolks
    1/4 cup lemon juice
    1/2 cup butter or margarine
    1/2 cup well-drained, grated cucumber

1. Beat egg yolks slightly in sauce pan.
2. Add lemon juice, ¼ cup butter; stir over low heat until blended.
3. Add remaining ¼ cup butter; continue cooking, stirring constantly, until thickened, smooth.
4. Stir in grated cucumber.
5. Serve over Salmon Casserole.
6. About 1 cup.

HORSERADISH SAUCE

    1 cup whipping cream
    1 tablespoon lemon juice
    1½ tablespoons bottled horseradish
    1/8 teaspoon salt

1. Whip cream; add remaining ingredients; blend thoroughly.
2. Serve with ham.
3. About 2½ cups.

BROWN GRAVY

1. Remove meat from pan; remove pan from heat.
2. Pour juice in pan into measuring cup.
3. Return 3 tablespoons of it to pan.
4. Add sufficient water to juice in cup to make 1 cup.
5. Add 2 tablespoons flour to juice in pan; blend.
6. Add liquid in cup; return to heat; cook slowly, stirring constantly until thickened and bubbly.
7. Add salt, pepper to taste.
8. About 1 cup.

BARBECUE SAUCE

    2 tablespoons butter or margarine
    1 onion, chopped fine
    1 clove garlic, minced
    1/2 cup chopped celery
    3/4 cup water
    1 cup ketchup
    2 tablespoons vinegar
    2 tablespoons lemon juice
    2 tablespoons Worcestershire sauce
    2 tablespoons brown sugar
    1 teaspoon dry mustard
    1 teaspoon salt
    1/4 teaspoon pepper

1. Melt butter in sauce pan; add onion, garlic, celery; cook until tender.
2. Add remaining ingredients; simmer 20 minutes.
3. About 2 cups.

RAISIN SAUCE

    1/2 cup brown sugar, firmly packed
    1½ teaspoons dry mustard
    1½ tablespoons flour
    1/2 cup seedless raisins
    1/4 cup vinegar
    1¾ cups water

1. Combine dry ingredients in sauce pan; add vinegar, water.
2. Cook 20 minutes over low heat.
3. Serve over ham or fresh pork.
4. About 2 cups.

ITALIAN SPAGHETTI SAUCE

⅓ cup minced onion
2 cloves of garlic, minced
3 tablespoons salad or olive oil
1 No. 2½ can Italian tomatoes
1 6-ounce can tomato paste
3 tomato paste cans of water
3 teaspoons salt
¼ teaspoon pepper
½ bay leaf

1. Sauté onion, garlic until golden brown in oil in sauce pan.
2. Add tomatoes, tomato paste, water, salt, pepper, bay leaf; blend; cover.
3. Simmer over very low heat 1¼ hours; stir occasionally.
4. Uncover; allow to simmer 1 hour longer.
5. Serve over cooked spaghetti with grated Parmesan cheese.
6. About six servings.

NOTE: Diced chicken livers, ground beef, diced mushrooms, lightly browned in oil may be added to sauce at start of cooking time.

MUSTARD SAUCE

1 tablespoon butter or margarine
2 tablespoons prepared mustard
2 teaspoons salt
2 teaspoons sugar
1 egg yolk, slightly beaten
1¼ cups cold water
2 tablespoons cold water
5 teaspoons cornstarch
1 tablespoon lemon juice

1. Melt butter in sauce pan.
2. Stir in mustard, salt, sugar.
3. Combine egg yolk, water; stir into butter mixture.
4. Mix remaining cold water, cornstarch to a smooth paste.
5. Stir into sauce; cook over low heat, stirring constantly, until thickened.
6. Remove from heat; add lemon juice.
7. Serve with ham.
8. About 1 cup.

WESTERN HERB SAUCE

¼ cup olive oil
¼ cup butter or margarine
2 tablespoons chopped scallions
1 8-ounce can sliced mushrooms, drained
2 tablespoons chopped chives
3 tablespoons chopped parsley
½ cup chopped walnuts
3 tablespoons bottled steak sauce
½ teaspoon salt
Dash pepper

1. Heat olive oil, butter in sauce pan; add scallions; mushrooms; sauté until lightly browned.
2. Add chives, parsley, walnuts, steak sauce, salt, pepper; blend well; simmer uncovered about 5 minutes.
3. Serve with steak, ground beef patties.
4. About 2 cups.

TARTAR SAUCE

1 cup mayonnaise
½ teaspoon minced onion
½ teaspoon chopped parsley
1 tablespoon chopped capers
1 tablespoon chopped cucumber pickles
1 tablespoon chopped green olives
1 teaspoon vinegar

1. Combine all ingredients; blend thoroughly.
2. Serve with broiled or fried fish or fried shrimp.
3. About 1½ cups.

GIBLET GRAVY

1. In sauce pan, simmer heart, liver, gizzard, neck, wing tips of fowl in 2½ cups salted water 30 minutes.
2. Remove giblets; chop fine; discard other pieces.
3. Melt 4 tablespoons fat in 10-inch broiler pan; add 4 tablespoons flour; blend.
4. Slowly add 2 cups stock from giblets; cook over low heat, stirring constantly until thickened; add chopped giblets.
5. Season to taste.
6. About 2½ cups.

SAUCES FOR DESSERTS

CHOCOLATE SAUCE

    1 15-ounce can sweetened
       condensed milk
    3 ounces unsweetened chocolate
    6 tablespoons hot water

1. Combine milk, chocolate, hot water in sauce pan.
2. Place over <u>low</u> heat; cook until thick, smooth, stirring constantly. If a thinner sauce is desired, add more hot water; stir until smooth.
3. Serve hot over Chocolate Brownies.
4. About 2 cups.

CUSTARD SAUCE

    2 cups milk
    3 eggs
    4 tablespoons sugar
    ¼ teaspoon salt
    1 teaspoon vanilla

1. Scald milk in sauce pan.
2. Beat eggs slightly; add sugar, salt; blend.
3. Add milk gradually, stirring constantly.
4. Return to sauce pan; cook over <u>low</u> heat, stirring constantly, until just slightly thickened—about 7-8 minutes.
5. Remove from heat; add vanilla.
6. About 2 cups.
NOTE: If overcooked, custard sauce will curdle: set in pan of cold water; beat with rotary beater until smooth.

RUM SAUCE

    2 eggs
    1 cup sugar
    1 cup whipping cream
    Rum flavoring

1. Beat eggs until stiff; add sugar slowly, continue beating until mixture loses its grain.
2. Whip cream until stiff; fold into egg mixture.
3. Add flavoring to taste.
4. Serve very cold over hot pudding.
5. About 1½ cups.

OLD FASHIONED LEMON SAUCE

    ½ cup butter or margarine
    1 cup sugar
    ¼ cup water
    1 egg, well beaten
    3 tablespoons lemon juice
    Grated rind of 1 lemon

1. Combine all ingredients in sauce pan.
2. Cook over <u>medium</u> heat, stirring constantly just until mixture comes to a boil.
3. Serve warm over gingerbread, steamed puddings.
4. About 1⅓ cups.

NUTMEG SAUCE

    ¼ cup butter or margarine
    ½ cup sugar
    1 egg yolk
    1½ tablespoons flour
    1 teaspoon vanilla
    1¼ cups boiling water
    ¼ teaspoon nutmeg

1. Cream butter in sauce pan; gradually add sugar; beat until light, fluffy.
2. Blend in egg yolk, flour, vanilla; gradually add boiling water.
3. Cook over <u>medium</u> heat, stirring constantly, until thickened.
4. Stir in nutmeg.
5. Serve warm over gingerbread, spice cake.
6. About 2 cups.

HARD SAUCE

    ⅓ cup butter or margarine
    1 cup sifted confectioners' sugar
    1 teaspoon vanilla or brandy
    Pinch salt

1. Cream butter until soft.
2. Add sugar gradually, continuing to cream until light, fluffy.
3. Add vanilla or brandy, salt; blend thoroughly.
4. Chill until needed.
5. Serve over steamed puddings, fruit cake, apple or mince pie.
6. About 1 cup.

The Pride

and Joy of Baking

W<small>E</small> Americans love desserts. Cakes and pies have long been our favorites. A beautiful cake or a home baked pie can be the grand finale of any meal. They make the simplest meal seem like a banquet, even provide a fitting climax for a more elaborate one. We like cookies too. They are good any time — lunch time, snack time, dinner time.

And, of course, there is nothing more tantalizing or mouth watering than the smell of something baking! Men love to brag about their wives' cakes and pies, so why not let your husband brag about you.

HOW TO BAKE A CAKE ON TOP OF THE RANGE

Unless recipe states otherwise, grease pan thoroughly. Pour cake batter into pan and cover

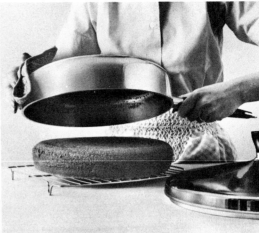

Place pan over <u>low</u> to <u>very low</u> heat
if using a mix .. or <u>medium</u> heat if using
a recipe.

A delicious cake ready for frosting.

HOW TO BAKE CAKE

PREPARED FROM A RECIPE:
1.   Unless recipe states otherwise, grease pan thoroughly. Pour batter into pan; cover.
2.   Place over <u>medium</u> heat 5 minutes. Reduce heat to <u>low</u>; bake time specified in
the recipe.

PREPARED FROM A SHORTENING TYPE MIX—YELLOW, WHITE OR FLAVORED:
1.   Use the 10-inch broiler pan and No. 843 cover for a full box of mix—the large two
layer cake size package. Use the No. 958 fry pan and cover for a half box of mix or the
small one layer cake size package.
2.   Prepare batter according to directions on the package. Pour batter into greased
pan;and cover. Place over <u>low</u> to <u>very low</u> heat depending on your range.
3.   BAKE: Two layer cake size (full box of mix) 40-50 minutes. One layer cake
size (half box of mix or small package) 20-25 minutes.
4.   Cake is done when toothpick inserted in center comes out clean and cake starts to
pull away from side of pan.
5.   Remove from heat; remove cover; let stand 5 minutes; turn out onto cake rack.

PREPARED FROM SPONGE TYPE MIX—ANGEL FOOD, SPONGE OR CHIFFON:
1.   Use round roaster pan fitted with No. 837 cake tube, No. 855 cover. Do not grease.
2.   Prepare batter according to directions on package. Pour batter into pan; run
spatula around sides and cut through batter to break any large air bubbles that may
have formed; cover. Place over <u>low</u> to <u>very low</u> heat.
3.   BAKE: 45-60 minutes or until top of cake springs back when pressed lightly
with a finger. Invert pan at once, resting handles on two cans, until cake is completely
cooled—at least 1½ hours.
4.   Loosen sides and bottom of cake from pan with a spatula; shake loose from tube.

70

WEAR-EVER NEW METHOD UTENSILS FOR BAKING

855 COVER

837 CAKE TUBE

854 PAN

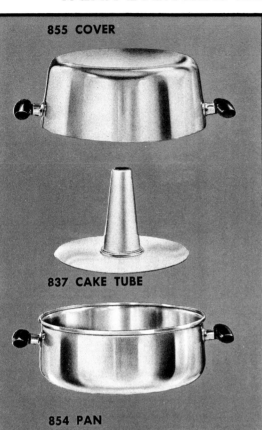

* 818 COVER

* 918 UTILITY PAN

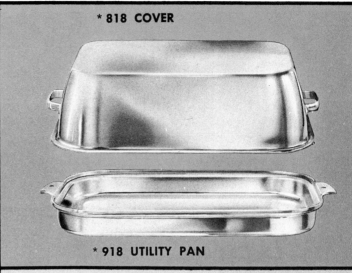

958 FRY PAN AND COVER

843 COVER

960 BROILER PAN

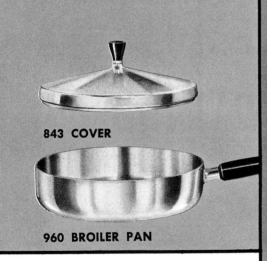

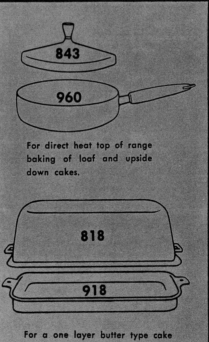

For direct heat top of range baking of loaf and upside down cakes.

For a one layer butter type cake

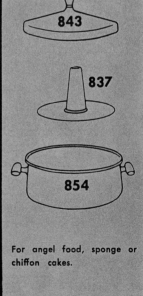

For angel food, sponge or chiffon cakes.

WEAR-EVER New Method Utensils can be used in many combinations, thus increasing their usefulness.

*No Inner-Clad

Margaret Mitchell's Favorite Baking Recipes

CAKES

PINEAPPLE UPSIDE DOWN CAKE

  ½ cup butter or margarine
  1 cup sugar
  2 eggs
  2 cups sifted cake flour
  3 teaspoons baking powder
  ½ teaspoon salt
  1 teaspoon vanilla
  ¾ cup cold water
  1 cup brown sugar, firmly packed
  ¼ cup butter or margarine
  5 slices pineapple
  5 maraschino cherries

1. Cream butter; add sugar; beat.
2. Add eggs, one at a time; beat well.
3. Sift flour, baking powder, salt together.
4. Add vanilla to water.
5. Alternately add dry and liquid ingredients; blend until smooth.
6. Grease 10-inch broiler pan; sprinkle with brown sugar; dot with remaining ¼ cup butter.
7. Arrange pineapple slices in pan; place cherry in center of each slice.
8. Spread cake batter evenly over pineapple; cover.
9. Place over <u>medium</u> heat 5 minutes.
10. Reduce heat to <u>low</u>; bake 50-55 minutes.
11. Allow to stand covered 5 minutes before turning cake upside down on platter.
12. Serve with whipped cream.

MAGGIE'S MAHOGANY CAKE

  ½ cup cocoa
  2 teaspoons baking soda
  ½ cup hot water
  ¾ cup butter or margarine
  1¾ cups sugar
  2 eggs
  1 teaspoon vanilla
  2½ cups sifted cake flour
  ½ teaspoon salt
  ¾ cup sour milk or buttermilk

1. Grease two 9 x 1½-inch layer cake pans; dust lightly with flour.
2. Mix cocoa, baking soda together; add hot water, stir until blended; set aside.
3. Cream butter until soft.
4. Add sugar gradually, continuing to cream until light, fluffy.
5. Add eggs, vanilla; beat thoroughly.
6. Sift flour, salt together.
7. Alternately add, in thirds, flour mixture, milk; beat well after each addition.
8. Add cocoa mixture; stir until blended.
9. Pour into pans; spread evenly.
10. Bake 35-40 minutes at 350°F.
11. When done, remove from oven; let stand 5 minutes.
12. Turn out onto cooling rack; turn, top side up; cool.
13. Spread Sea Foam Frosting, page 74, between layers, over top, sides of cake.

NOTE: This is a very large and very special type cake. It is best baked in the oven.

72

BLACK WALNUT CAKE

  ½ cup butter or margarine
1½ cups sugar
  3 eggs
  ½ cup black walnuts, ground
  1 teaspoon black walnut extract
  ¾ teaspoon vanilla
  3 cups sifted cake flour
  3 teaspoons baking powder
  ½ teaspoon salt
  1 cup milk

1. Grease two 9 x 1½-inch layer cake pans; dust lightly with flour.
2. Cream butter until soft.
3. Add sugar gradually, continuing to cream until light, fluffy.
4. Add eggs, black walnuts, black walnut extract, vanilla; beat thoroughly.
5. Sift flour, baking powder, salt together.
6. Alternately add in thirds, flour mixture, milk; beat well after each addition.
7. Pour into pans; spread evenly.
8. Bake 25-30 minutes at 375°F.
9. When done, remove from oven; let stand 5 minutes.
10. Turn out onto cooling rack; turn, top side up; cool.
11. Spread Fluffy Frosting between layers, over top, sides of cake.
12. Sprinkle with chopped black walnuts.

COCONUT SILVER CAKE

  ½ cup butter or margarine
  1 cup sugar
  1 teaspoon vanilla
  2 cups sifted cake flour
  2 teaspoons baking powder
  ½ teaspoon salt
  ⅔ cup milk
  3 stiffly beaten egg whites

1. Cream butter; add sugar, vanilla; cream until light, fluffy.
2. Sift together dry ingredients; add alternately with milk; mix well.
3. Fold in stiffly beaten egg whites.
4. Put into greased 10-inch broiler pan; cover.
5. Place over medium heat 5 minutes.
6. Reduce heat to low; bake 40-45 minutes.
7. When cool spread with Fluffy Frosting, page 74; sprinkle with coconut.

BUTTER CREAM CAKE

  ⅓ cup butter or margarine
  1 cup sugar
  2 eggs
  2 cups sifted cake flour
  2 teaspoons baking powder
  ½ teaspoon salt
  1 teaspoon vanilla
  ⅔ cup milk

1. Cream butter; add sugar; beat.
2. Add eggs, one at time; beat well.
3. Sift flour, baking powder, salt together.
4. Add vanilla to milk.
5. Alternately add dry and liquid ingredients; blend until smooth.
6. Put into greased 10-inch broiler pan; cover.
7. Place over medium heat 5 minutes.
8. Reduce heat to low; bake 40-45 minutes.
9. Frost as desired.

PRIZE SPICE CAKE

  6 tablespoons shortening
  1 cup brown sugar, firmly packed
  2 eggs
1½ cups sifted cake flour
  ½ teaspoon baking powder
  ¼ teaspoon salt
  ¼ teaspoon cloves
  ½ teaspoon nutmeg
  1 teaspoon cinnamon
  ½ teaspoon vanilla
  ¾ teaspoon baking soda
  ½ cup sour milk or buttermilk

1. Cream shortening; add sugar; beat.
2. Add eggs, one at a time; beat well.
3. Sift dry ingredients together except soda.
4. Add vanilla, soda to sour milk.
5. Alternately add dry and liquid ingredients; blend until smooth.
6. Pour into greased 10-inch broiler pan; cover.
7. Place over medium heat 5 minutes.
8. Reduce heat to low; bake 25-30 minutes.
9. Frost as desired.

CREAM SPONGE CAKE

    4 egg whites
    ½ cup sugar
    4 egg yolks
    2 tablespoons cold water
    1 teaspoon vanilla
    ½ cup sugar
    1 cup sifted cake flour
    1½ tablespoons cornstarch
    1¼ teaspoons baking powder
    ¼ teaspoon salt

1. Beat egg whites until stiff, but not dry; add sugar; beat thoroughly.
2. Beat egg yolks, water, vanilla until lemon colored; add sugar; beat until well blended.
3. Fold two mixtures together.
4. Sift dry ingredients together; fold into mixture with wooden spoon.
5. Pour into ungreased 10-inch broiler pan; cover.
6. Place over medium heat 5 minutes.
7. Reduce heat to low; bake 45-50 minutes.
8. Frost as desired.

ANGEL FOOD CAKE

    1 cup sifted cake flour
    1¼ cups sugar
    ¼ teaspoon salt
    1 cup egg whites
    ¾ teaspoon cream of tartar
    1 teaspoon vanilla
    ¼ teaspoon almond extract

1. Sift flour, sugar, salt together nine times.
2. Beat egg whites with wire whip until frothy.
3. Add cream of tartar; continue beating until eggs are stiff but not dry; add vanilla, almond extract; beat one minute longer.
4. Fold in dry ingredients, about 4 tablespoons at a time, using a wooden spoon. Fold only until dry ingredients disappear in mixture.
5. Pour into ungreased round roaster fitted with cake tube; cover.
6. Bake over very low heat one hour or until done.

BUTTER CREAM ICING

    1 tablespoon butter or margarine
    1 cup confectioners' sugar
    1 tablespoon milk
    1 teaspoon vanilla

1. Melt butter in sauce pan; add sugar, milk, vanilla.
2. Beat well; spread on cake.
VARIATIONS:
Chocolate Cream Icing: Add 1 square melted unsweetened chocolate.
Orange Cream Icing: Substitute orange juice for one-half milk; add ½ teaspoon grated orange peel.

FLUFFY FROSTING

    2 egg whites, unbeaten
    1½ cups sugar
    5 tablespoons cold water
    1½ teaspoons white corn syrup
    1 teaspoon vanilla

1. Combine egg whites, sugar, water, corn syrup; beat until thoroughly blended.
2. Place over rapidly boiling water.
3. Beat constantly with hand or electric beater until frosting will stand in peaks on beater.
4. Remove from heat; add vanilla; blend.
VARIATIONS:
Marshmallow Frosting: After removing from heat, fold in 6-8 quartered marshmallows or 4 tablespoons marshmallow creme.
Chocolate Frosting: Melt 3 squares unsweetened chocolate; cool slightly. Gently fold chocolate into frosting after removing from heat.
Sea Foam Frosting: Substitute 1½ cups brown sugar, firmly packed, for granulated sugar; omit corn syrup; add speck of salt.
Orange Mist Frosting: Substitute orange juice for water, add 1 tablespoon grated orange rind; omit vanilla.
Peppermint Frosting: Substitute few drops peppermint for vanilla. Tint pale green or pink, or fold in ½ cup crushed peppermint stick candy.

PIES

FLAKY PASTRY

> 2¼ cups sifted all purpose flour
> 1 teaspoon salt
> ¾ cup shortening, lard or vegetable
> 3-4 tablespoons cold water

1. Sift flour, salt together into bowl.
2. Cut in shortening with pastry blender or 2 knives until mixture resembles coarse meal; continue cutting until particles start to cling together in little balls about the size of peas.
3. Mark mixture off into thirds with fork.
4. Sprinkle about 1 tablespoon water on one part; quickly work it in with fork.
5. Repeat operation on each part until particles will cling together when pressed between fingers. Dough should not be wet or sticky. The amount of water may vary with flour but always use as little as possible. Empty contents of bowl onto Alcoa Wrap.
6. Place hands under foil, cup fashion; press dough into ball; wrap; chill 10-15 minutes before rolling.
7. Sprinkle board or pastry cloth lightly with flour. Run rolling pin over board or cloth once or twice.
8. Divide ball of prepared pastry into two parts.
9. Place one part in center of board; flatten slightly with rolling pin.
10. With quick light strokes, roll from center out to form circle about ⅛-inch thick and 1½-inches larger than inverted pan. If edge splits or cracks, pinch together. Pastry may be given a quarter turn to loosen but do not turn it over. Use as little flour as possible during the rolling as excess flour will toughen the crust.
11. Fold in half, then in half again. Place in ungreased pan with point of dough in center; unfold.
12. Fit gently into pan removing all air bubbles.

For Double Crust Pie

1. Prepare and add filling according to recipe.
2. Roll second part of dough same as first part into a 12-inch circle; fold in half; make several slits in center for steam to escape; place over filling; unfold.
3. Lift up edge of bottom crust and press edge of top crust under it to make a stand-up edge.
4. Place right index finger on inside of edge; with left thumb and index finger, pinch pastry at that point; repeat around edge, then repinch to sharpen points.
5. For a shiny finish, brush top crust and edge with milk or ice water.
6. Bake as directed in recipe.

For Single Shell Pie—unbaked

1. Prepare crust same as above using 1½ cups sifted all purpose flour, ½ teaspoon salt, ½ cup shortening and 2-3 tablespoons cold water.
2. Fit into pan; fold overhang under to form stand up edge; crimp edge.
3. Add filling; bake as directed in recipe.

For Single Shell Pie—baked

1. Prepare Single Shell; fit into pan; finish edge.
2. Prick bottom and sides closely and deeply with a fork.
3. Bake 12-15 minutes at 450°F. If bubbles appear during baking, prick them several times.

FRESH RHUBARB PIE

　　Flaky Pastry
3　cups unpeeled rhubarb, diced
1　cup sugar
1　egg, beaten
2　tablespoons flour
　　Juice of ½ lemon
2　tablespoons butter or margarine

1. Line ungreased 9-inch pie pan with pastry.
2. Brush with slightly beaten egg white.
3. Combine rhubarb, sugar, egg, flour, lemon juice; blend.
4. Pour into pastry-lined pan; dot with butter.
5. Adjust top crust.
6. Bake 45-50 minutes at 400°F.
7. Serve with wedge of sharp cheese or sprinkled with confectioners' sugar.
8. Six servings.

SOUTHERN PECAN PIE

　　Flaky Pastry—Unbaked Shell
½　cup butter or margarine
½　cup sugar
¾　cup white corn syrup
2　tablespoons strained honey
3　eggs, slightly beaten
1　teaspoon vanilla
2　cups pecans

1. Line ungreased 9-inch pie pan with pastry.
2. Cream butter until soft.
3. Add sugar gradually, continuing to cream until light, fluffy.
4. Stir in slowly, syrup, honey, eggs, vanilla, 1 cup nuts.
5. Pour into shell; place remaining 1 cup nuts on top.
6. Bake 50-55 minutes at 350°F.; cool.
7. Spread with sweetened whipped cream before serving.
8. Six servings.

MAGGIE'S LEMON PIE

　　Flaky Pastry—Baked 9-inch Shell
2　cups sugar
4　tablespoons cornstarch
5　tablespoons flour
½　teaspoon salt
2　cups boiling water
4　tablespoons butter or margarine
4　egg yolks, beaten
2　lemons, juice and grated rind

1. Combine sugar, cornstarch, flour, salt in No. 802 inner pan.
2. Add boiling water, slowly, stirring constantly; add butter.
3. Bring 1 quart water to boil in round roaster; insert steamer ring; add inner pan; cook 30 minutes, or until clear and thickened; stir several times.
4. Add egg yolks, lemon juice, rind; blend; cook 10 minutes longer, stirring twice; cool.
5. Pour into baked shell.
6. Cover with Meringue.
7. Bake 8-10 minutes at 400°F. until delicately browned.
8. Six servings.
TO MAKE MERINGUE: Beat two egg whites until they form soft peaks. Add 4 tablespoons sugar gradually, continuing to beat until stiff but not dry.

LIBBY'S PUMPKIN PIE

　　Flaky Pastry—Unbaked Shell
2　eggs, slightly beaten
1¾　cups canned pumpkin
¾　cup sugar
½　teaspoon salt
1　teaspoon cinnamon
½　teaspoon ginger
¼　teaspoon cloves
1⅔　cups evaporated milk, whole milk
　　or light cream

1. Line ungreased 9-inch pie pan with pastry.
2. Combine eggs, pumpkin, sugar, salt, cinnamon, ginger, cloves, milk; blend thoroughly.
3. Pour into shell.
4. Bake 15 minutes at 425°F.; reduce temperature to 350°F.; bake 45 minutes longer.
5. Serve with sweetened whipped cream.
6. Six servings.

RAISIN PIE

    Flaky Pastry
   3 cups seedless raisins
   3 cups water
  ½ teaspoon grated lemon rind
  ⅔ cup sugar
   3 tablespoons flour
  ¼ teaspoon cinnamon
   1 tablespoon butter or margarine

1. Line ungreased 9-inch pie pan with pastry.
2. Combine raisins, water, lemon rind in sauce pan; bring to boil; boil 5 minutes.
3. Combine sugar, flour, cinnamon; add sufficient juice from raisins to make smooth paste; stir; add to raisins.
4. Cook over <u>low</u> heat, stirring constantly until thickened, clear—about 5 minutes.
5. Add butter; cool.
6. Pour into pastry-lined pan.
7. Adjust top crust.
8. Bake 30-35 minutes at 425°F.
9. Sprinkle with confectioners' sugar before serving.
10. Six servings.

FRESH APPLE PIE

    Flaky Pastry
  ⅔ cup sugar
  ¼ teaspoon nutmeg
  ¼ teaspoon cinnamon
  ⅛ teaspoon salt
   1 teaspoon lemon juice
   6 cups pared, cored ¼-inch apple slices
   1 tablespoon butter or margarine

1. Line ungreased 9-inch pie pan with pastry.
2. Brush with slightly beaten egg white.
3. Combine sugar, nutmeg, cinnamon, salt, lemon juice; add apples; mix well; put into pastry lined pan.
4. Dot with butter.
5. Adjust top crust.
6. Bake 40-45 minutes at 425°F.
7. Serve slightly warm with wedge of sharp cheese or with vanilla ice cream or sprinkled with confectioners' sugar.
8. Six servings.

FRESH BERRY PIE

    Flaky Pastry
  ⅔ cup sugar
   2 tablespoons flour
  ¼ teaspoon nutmeg
  ¼ teaspoon cinnamon
  ⅛ teaspoon salt
   1 teaspoon lemon juice
   4 cups blackberries or black raspberries
   1 tablespoon butter or margarine

1. Line ungreased 9-inch pie pan with pastry.
2. Brush with slightly beaten egg white.
3. Combine sugar, flour, nutmeg, cinnamon, salt, lemon juice, berries; blend thoroughly.
4. Pour into pastry lined pan; dot with butter.
5. Adjust top crust.
6. Bake 40-45 minutes at 425°F.
7. Six servings.

CHOCOLATE CREAM PIE

    Flaky Pastry—Baked 9-inch Shell
 1½ cups sugar
  ½ teaspoon salt
 2½ tablespoons cornstarch
   1 tablespoon flour
   3 cups milk
   3 squares unsweetened chocolate, shaved
   3 egg yolks, slightly beaten
   1 tablespoon butter or margarine
 1½ teaspoons vanilla

1. Combine sugar, salt, cornstarch, flour in sauce pan.
2. Add milk gradually; stir until mixed; stir in chocolate.
3. Cook over <u>medium</u> heat, stirring constantly until mixture thickens, boils; boil 1 minute.
4. Remove from heat; stir a little of mixture into egg yolks; blend into hot mixture.
5. Return to heat; bring to boil; boil 1 minute longer; remove from heat.
6. Stir in butter, vanilla; cool.
7. Pour into baked shell.
8. Spread with sweetened whipped cream; top with chopped nuts.
9. Six servings.

COOKIES

DATE NUT PINWHEELS

2¼ cups pitted dates, cut into small
    pieces
  1 cup sugar
  1 cup water
  1 cup nuts, chopped
  1 cup shortening
  2 cups brown sugar, firmly packed
  3 eggs
  4 cups sifted all purpose flour
  ½ teaspoon salt
  ½ teaspoon baking soda

1. Combine dates, sugar, water in sauce pan; bring to boil; cook over low heat 10 minutes or until thick; add nuts; cool.
2. Cream shortening until soft.
3. Add sugar gradually, continuing to cream until light, fluffy.
4. Add eggs; beat well.
5. Sift flour, salt, baking soda together; add in 2 additions; beat well after each addition.
6. Shape dough into ball; wrap in Alcoa Wrap; chill several hours.
7. When dough is very firm, divide into two parts.
8. Roll each part into rectangle ⅛-inch thick.
9. Spread each with date-nut mixture.
10. Roll each part up, jelly roll fashion; wrap in Alcoa Wrap.
11. Place in refrigerator; chill several hours or overnight.
12. Cut into ¼-inch slices; place on ungreased cookie sheet.
13. Bake 10-12 minutes at 375°F.
14. About 5 dozen cookies.

BLACK WALNUT COOKIES

1½ cups black walnuts
1½ cups shredded coconut
1¾ cups butter or margarine
  1 pound brown sugar
  ½ cup granulated sugar
  2 eggs
  1 teaspoon vanilla
  1 teaspoon black walnut extract
  6 cups sifted cake flour
  1 teaspoon cream of tartar
  1 teaspoon salt
  ½ teaspoon baking soda

1. Grind nuts, coconut together in food chopper.
2. Cream butter until soft.
3. Add sugars gradually, continuing to cream until light, fluffy.
4. Add eggs, vanilla, black walnut extract, ground nuts, coconut; beat well.
5. Sift flour, cream of tartar, salt, baking soda together; add in 3 additions; beat well after each addition.
6. Shape into rolls, 2 inches in diameter; wrap in Alcoa Wrap.
7. Place in refrigerator; chill several hours or overnight.
8. Slice thin; place on ungreased cookie sheet.
9. Bake 10-12 minutes at 375°F.
10. About 12 dozen cookies.

NOTE: All or part of this dough may be frozen for later use.

ROB ROY COOKIES

    1 cup shortening
1½ cups brown sugar, firmly packed
    1 teaspoon salt
    ½ teaspoon cinnamon
    ½ teaspoon cloves
    ¼ cup buttermilk
    2 eggs, unbeaten
1¾ cups sifted all purpose flour
    ¾ teaspoon baking soda
1½ cups uncooked rolled oats
    1 cup chopped nuts
    1 cup seedless raisins

1. Cream shortening until soft.
2. Add sugar gradually, continuing to cream until light, fluffy.
3. Add salt, spices, milk, eggs; blend thoroughly.
4. Sift flour, baking soda together; add in two parts.
5. Add oats, nuts, raisins; blend thoroughly.
6. Drop by level tablespoon 2-inches apart onto ungreased cookie sheet: press flat.
7. Bake 10-15 minutes at 375°F.
8. About 5 dozen cookies.

CHOCOLATE CHIP COOKIES

    ½ cup butter or margarine
    ½ cup granulated sugar
    ¼ cup brown sugar, firmly packed
    1 egg
    1 teaspoon vanilla
    1 cup sifted cake flour
    ½ teaspoon salt
    ½ teaspoon baking soda
    ½ cup nuts, chopped
    1 6-ounce package semi-sweet chocolate bits

1. Cream butter until soft.
2. Add sugars gradually, continuing to cream until light, fluffy.
3. Add egg, vanilla; beat well.
4. Sift flour, salt, baking soda together; add; beat until smooth.
5. Fold in nuts, chocolate bits.
6. Drop from teaspoon, 2 inches apart, onto ungreased cookie sheet.
7. Bake 10-12 minutes at 375°F.
8. About 4 dozen cookies.

MAGGIE'S CHOCOLATE BROWNIES

    1 cup plus 2 tablespoons butter or margarine
    6 squares unsweetened chocolate, melted
2¼ cups sugar
    5 eggs, beaten
    2 teaspoons vanilla
1¾ cups sifted cake flour
    1 teaspoon salt
1½ cups walnuts or pecans, chopped

1. Melt butter, chocolate in sauce pan.
2. Add sugar, eggs, vanilla; beat thoroughly.
3. Sift flour, salt together; add; beat until smooth.
4. Fold in nuts.
5. Pour into greased utility pan; spread evenly; cover with No. 818 cover.
6. Bake on top of range over _medium_ heat 5 minutes; reduce heat to _low_; continue baking 20-25 minutes.
7. Cool slightly; cut into 2-inch squares. These brownies have a shiny surface and fudge-like center.
8. About 3 dozen squares.

COTTAGE CHEESE COOKIE STICKS

    1 cup cream-style cottage cheese
    1 cup butter or margarine
    2 cups sifted all purpose flour
    ¼ cup melted butter or margarine
    ¾ cup brown sugar, firmly packed
    ¾ cup nuts, chopped fine

1. Blend cottage cheese, the one cup butter together with pastry blender.
2. Blend sifted flour into mixture until dough holds together.
3. Roll out on lightly floured board to ⅛-inch thickness.
4. Brush melted butter over dough; sprinkle brown sugar, nuts over entire surface.
5. Cut into equal strips, about 3 inches wide; cut each strip into triangles, each about 3 inches wide at the base.
6. Beginning at base of triangle, roll dough into sticks; place on greased cookie sheet, point side down.
7. Bake 20 minutes at 400°F., or until golden brown.
8. About 4½ dozen cookie sticks.

BREADS

FRENCH TOAST

  2 eggs
  2 tablespoons sugar
½ teaspoon salt
  1 cup milk
  1 tablespoon melted shortening
  6 slices stale bread

1. Break eggs into bowl; beat well.
2. Add sugar, salt, milk, shortening.
3. Dip bread into mixture.
4. Heat utility pan over medium-high heat until a piece of white paper placed in bottom of pan starts to turn brown.
5. Remove paper; reduce heat to medium; brown toast on both sides.
6. Serve either with confectioners' sugar or syrup.
7. Two-three servings.

SCOTCH SCONES

  2 cups sifted all purpose flour
  4 teaspoons baking powder
  1 teaspoon salt
  4 tablespoons shortening
⅔ cup milk

1. Sift dry ingredients together.
2. Cut in shortening with pastry blender or two knives; add milk to make soft dough.
3. Toss on floured board; pat into two round patties; roll ½ inch thick.
4. Cut each patty into six triangular sections.
5. Heat utility pan over medium-high heat until a small piece of white paper placed in bottom starts to turn brown; reduce heat to medium-low.
6. Bake scones until delicately browned on both sides. Allow 7-9 minutes per side.
7. Twelve scones.

CORN BREAD

1¼ cups sifted all purpose flour
  1 tablespoon baking powder
  1 teaspoon salt
  1 tablespoon sugar
  1 cup corn meal (yellow or white)
  1 egg, beaten
  1 cup milk
  2 tablespoons melted shortening

1. Sift flour, baking powder, salt, sugar together; add corn meal; mix well.
2. Combine egg, milk, shortening; add to dry ingredients; mix.
3. Pour into greased 10-inch broiler pan; cover; bake over low heat 25-30 minutes.
4. Cut into wedges; serve hot.

GRIDDLE CAKES

1¼ cups sifted all purpose flour
2½ teaspoons baking powder
  3 tablespoons sugar
¾ teaspoon salt
  1 egg
  1 cup milk
  3 tablespoons butter or margarine, melted

1. Sift dry ingredients together.
2. Beat egg; add milk.
3. Stir into dry ingredients; mix.
4. Add melted butter.
5. Heat utility pan over medium-high heat until a piece of white paper placed in bottom starts to turn brown.
6. Remove paper; reduce heat to medium; pour cakes.
7. Brown on one side; turn; brown on other side.
8. About 10 medium-size cakes.

HUNGARIAN COFFEE CAKE

- 2 cakes compressed yeast
- 1 cup milk
- ½ cup sugar
- 1 teaspoon salt
- 2 eggs, well beaten
- 4½ – 4¾ cups sifted all purpose flour
- ½ cup shortening, melted
- ½ cup melted butter or margarine
- 1¼ cups sugar
- 2 teaspoons cinnamon
- ¾ cup finely chopped nuts
- 1 cup raisins

1. Crumble yeast into mixing bowl.
2. Scald milk in sauce pan; cool to lukewarm; add to yeast.
3. Add sugar, salt; let stand until thoroughly dissolved.
4. Add eggs; mix well.
5. Add ½ of the flour; beat until smooth, very elastic.
6. Add melted, cooled shortening.
7. Add remainder of flour—just enough so dough is soft, workable.
8. Round off and set to rise in a greased bowl in warm place until dough is double in bulk.
9. Punch dough down; divide in half; cut into pieces the size of walnuts; form into balls.
10. Roll each ball in melted butter; then in combined sugar, cinnamon, nuts.
11. Place one layer balls in greased 10 x 4-inch tube pan so that they barely touch.
12. Sprinkle with a few raisins.
13. Add another layer of balls, sprinkle more raisins in crevices; repeat, using all dough, raisins.
14. Cover; let rise in warm place until light (about 45 minutes).
15. Bake 35-40 minutes at 375°F.
16. Loosen from pan with spatula; invert.
17. To serve, break apart.
18. Eight servings.

CURRY BISCUITS

- 2 cups sifted all purpose flour
- 3 teaspoons baking powder
- ½ teaspoon salt
- ½ teaspoon curry powder
- ¼ cup shortening
- ⅔ cup milk (approximate)

1. Sift flour, baking powder, salt, curry powder together.
2. Cut in shortening until mixture resembles corn meal.
3. Make a well in center of mixture; add almost all milk; stir until soft dough is formed, adding remaining milk if necessary.
4. Knead dough gently on lightly floured board about 30 seconds.
5. Pat out to ½-inch thickness; cut into small biscuits; place on top of Veal Casserole, page 61; bake as directed.

CARAWAY LOAF

- ½ cup butter or margarine
- 1 cup sugar
- 2 eggs
- 2 teaspoons caraway seed
- 2 cups sifted all purpose flour
- 1½ teaspoons baking powder
- ½ teaspoon salt
- ½ teaspoon mace
- ½ cup milk

1. Cream butter, sugar until light, fluffy.
2. Add eggs, one at a time, beating after each addition.
3. Add caraway seeds; blend.
4. Sift flour, baking powder, salt, mace together.
5. Alternately add in thirds—flour mixture, milk; blend well after each addition.
6. Pour into greased 9 x 5 x 3-inch loaf pan.
7. Bake 60 minutes at 350°F.
8. One loaf.

BUTTER CRUMB DUMPLINGS

    1 cup sifted all purpose flour
    2 teaspoons baking powder
    2 teaspoons poppy seeds
    ½ teaspoon celery salt
    ½ teaspoon poultry seasoning
    1 teaspoon dried onion flakes
    1 tablespoon salad oil
    ½ cup milk
    2 tablespoons butter or margarine, melted
    1 cup soft bread crumbs

1. Combine flour, baking powder, poppy seeds, celery salt, poultry seasoning, onion flakes.
2. Combine oil, milk; add to flour mixture; beat until smooth.
3. Stir melted butter into crumbs; spread out on sheet of Alcoa Wrap.
4. Drop dough by tablespoons in 8 equal portions into buttered crumbs; roll around to coat with crumbs.
5. Place on top of Perfect Casserole, page 61; bake as directed.

CRANBERRY BREAD

    2 cups sifted all purpose flour
    1 cup sugar
    1½ teaspoons baking powder
    1 teaspoon salt
    ½ teaspoon baking soda
    1 tablespoon grated orange rind
    Juice of 1 orange
    2 tablespoons shortening
    1 egg, well beaten
    1 cup chopped walnuts
    1 cup raw cranberries, cut in half

1. Sift flour, sugar, baking powder, salt, baking soda together into large mixing bowl.
2. Combine orange juice with enough boiling water to measure ¾ cup; add shortening; stir until dissolved; blend in egg.
3. Add to dry ingredients; mix until all dry particles are moistened.
4. Stir in nuts, cranberries, orange rind.
5. Turn into greased 9 x 5 x 3-inch loaf pan.
6. Bake 55-65 minutes at 350°F.; cool before slicing.
7. One loaf.

LEMON BREAD

    6 tablespoons butter or margarine
    1 cup sugar
    2 eggs, beaten
    ½ cup milk
    Grated rind of 1 lemon
    1½ cups sifted all purpose flour
    1 teaspoon baking powder
    ¼ teaspoon salt
    1½ cups chopped pecans
    ⅓ cup sugar
    Juice of 1 lemon

1. Cream together butter, sugar; add eggs, milk, lemon rind; beat thoroughly.
2. Sift together flour, baking powder, salt.
3. Spoon dry ingredients into creamed mixture; add pecans; mix quickly.
4. Pour batter into greased 8 x 4 x 2½-inch foil loaf pan.
5. Bake 55-60 minutes at 350°F.
6. Combine sugar, lemon juice; pour over bread immediately after removing from oven.
7. Cool bread in pan.
8. One small loaf.

JEAN'S BAKING POWDER BISCUITS

    2 cups sifted all purpose flour
    4 teaspoons baking powder
    ½ teaspoon salt
    ½ teaspoon cream of tartar
    2 teaspoons sugar
    ½ cup shortening
    ⅔ cup milk

1. Sift flour, baking powder, salt, cream of tartar, sugar together three times.
2. Put in bowl; cut in shortening until consistency of coarse cornmeal.
3. Make a well in center; pour in milk; stir with fork just until dough clings together.
4. Turn out on lightly floured board; knead very gently 8-10 times.
5. Roll to ½-inch thickness; cut; brush with milk.
6. Bake 10-12 minutes at 450°F.
7. About 12 biscuits.

VARIATION:
Savory Biscuits: Add 1 tablespoon each minced onion, parsley to dry ingredients.

PLAIN MUFFINS

  2 cups sifted all purpose flour
  2 tablespoons sugar
  3 teaspoons baking powder
  1 teaspoon salt
  1 cup milk
  1 egg, beaten
  3 tablespoons melted shortening

1. Sift dry ingredients together.
2. Combine milk, egg.
3. Pour liquid ingredients into dry ingredients.
4. Stir only until flour is moistened.
5. Stir in melted shortening.
6. Fill greased muffin pans ⅔ full.
7. Bake 20 minutes at 425°F.
8. Twelve muffins.

PARTY BISCUITS

  3 cups biscuit mix
  ¼ cup melted shortening or oil
  1 10½-ounce can condensed cream
    of mushroom soup, undiluted

1. Combine biscuit mix, shortening, soup; blend thoroughly.
2. Turn out on lightly floured board; knead 8 to 10 times.
3. Roll or pat to ½-inch thickness; cut.
4. Bake 10-12 minutes at 450°F.
5. About 18-20 biscuits.

DESSERT SUGGESTIONS

Angel food cake slices topped with sweetened whipped cream and fresh strawberries.

Chocolate brownie squares topped with peppermint or pistachio ice cream and chocolate sauce.

Plain cream puff shells (order from bakery) filled with vanilla ice cream, topped with chocolate sauce.

Left-over white or yellow cake slices topped with canned cherry pie filling.

Fresh or canned fruit with a cookie.

Fruit cake or canned fig or plum pudding topped with rum sauce.

Lemon sherbet topped with Creme de Menthe.

Toasted crackers with Roquefort, Liederkranz, Camembert or Swiss Gruyere Cheese.

Honeydew melon wedges with clusters of white seedless grapes.

Packaged puddings in tart shells or sherbet glasses with whipped cream or a substitute.

Vanilla ice cream balls rolled in chopped nuts with caramel sauce.

Stale cookies put through food press and blended with chopped nuts makes a good topping for ice cream or prepared puddings.

Canned fruit cocktail molded in strawberry or cherry gelatin.

Spice cake or gingerbread with lemon sauce.

When

You Entertain

WHEN you entertain whether it's having the girls in for lunch or the gang for a buffet supper, you want your party to be a success.

Successful parties are those that seem to move along with practically no effort on the part of the hostess. Such an effect is not an accident, but the direct result of very careful planning and organization. And therein lies the magic formula every successful hostess follows.

THE MENU

First comes the planning of the menu. What you serve depends to some extent on the occasion, the time of the day and the season of the year. It may be a variation of a menu you have used before or built around some dish you prepare especially well. It should never contain anything you haven't made before. It need not be elaborate. Simple foods, well prepared and attractively served, are preferable.

Avoid dishes that require a lot of last minute preparation or that can't be kept waiting. A casserole dish such as Shrimp Harpin, which may be prepared early in the day then baked while guests are arriving, is a good choice. Veal Paprika is a delicious roast that can be started ahead of time. It carves easily and doesn't mind waiting if some of the guests are late. The same rule applies to the dessert. Plan something that can be prepared early in the day or even the day before.

Once the menu is planned the next step is to prepare the market order. Check each recipe to be certain you will have everything you need. Do the marketing the day before the party rather than the day of the party.

A WRITTEN WORK SCHEDULE IS A MUST. Carefully planned and meticulously followed it helps to avoid last minute flurry. It also gives you the assurance your party will be a success. The most priceless compliment you can receive is for a guest to say, "Mary, your party was simply perfect. I don't know how you manage to do things so easily."

This work schedule should be prepared in two parts—things to do before the day of the party and those to be done the day of the party.

Part one of your schedule will include the checking of table and serving accessories to be certain that linens, china, glassware and silver are clean and sparkling. Any special cleaning you think is necessary should be listed. Anything you may need to borrow from a neighbor or friend, such as extra chairs or little tables, should be noted. Everything that can be done ahead of time should be listed.

The second part of your work schedule is for the day of the party. If entertaining is relatively new to you, plan it on an hourly basis, getting as much as possible taken care of early in the day. Lastly, but so important is the time you allot to yourself. This is the time to dress carefully, make a last minute check to be sure everything is in readiness.

Then assured all is well, you greet your guests confident your party will be one long remembered.

BRUNCHES

A brunch is a late breakfast and an early lunch combined into one meal. It may be served anytime between 10:30 and 1 o'clock any day of the week. It is a simple informal meal, frequently served buffet style and an ideal way to entertain.

MENU SUGGESTIONS: Chilled Fruit Juice—Scrambled Eggs with Little Sausages—Hashed Browned Potatoes—Rolls—Coffee Cake—Coffee

Melon Balls—French Toast with Red Raspberry Jam—Crisp Bacon—Coffee

Grapefruit—Quartered Hard Cooked Eggs and Asparagus Spears topped with Deviled Ham Sauce—Toast—Lemon Bread—Jam—Coffee

Frosted Apricot Nectar—Chicken Livers Saute on Rice—Broiled Tomato Half—Toasted English Muffins—Jam—Coffee

LUNCHEONS

The party luncheon holds top honors as woman's favorite mode of entertaining. Since most luncheons are strictly feminine affairs and just about everyone is diet-conscious, it is wise to plan a simple rather than an elaborate menu.

MENU SUGGESTIONS: Fresh Fruit Salad Plate—Cream Cheese blended with Crumbled Cooked Bacon on Raisin Bread Sandwich—Salted Nuts—Coffee

Creamed Chicken on Toast topped with grated sharp cheese slipped under the broiler until bubbly and topped with crisp crumbled bacon—Pickles, Olives—Small Cake Square—Coffee

Salmon Casserole with Lemon Cucumber Sauce—Crusty Rolls—Chocolate Brownies—Coffee

BUFFET MEALS

Serving food from a buffet table is a most delightful way to entertain ten or more guests. The affair may be a brunch, a luncheon, a dinner, a late supper or even a small wedding reception. It can be informal or done with a touch of elegance depending on the occasion.

The menu is simple—one or two hot dishes or a hot and a cold dish, a salad or relish tray and hot buttered rolls—all foods that can be eaten without the use of a knife. Dessert and coffee may be served later from the same table or a small separate table. The only strict rule that should be followed is to be sure each guest has a place to put his plate after he has served himself. Men especially dislike balancing a plate of food on their knees.

MENU SUGGESTIONS: Tamale Rice with Frankfurters—Molded Fruit Salad—Hot Buttered Rolls —Cake Squares—Coffee

Glazed Ham Balls—Buttered Lima Beans—Relish Tray—Buttered Rolls—Cherry Pie made with canned Cherry Pie Filling—Coffee

Barbecued Spareribs—Frozen French Fries heated and made crisp—Tossed Green Salad— Garlic Bread—Lemon Sherbet topped with Creme de Menthe—Coffee

Fried Chicken—Small New Potatoes and Peas in Cream Sauce—Peach Halves filled with Orange Marmalade—Hot Buttered Rolls—Chocolate Brownies topped with Peppermint Stick Ice Cream and Chocolate Sauce—Coffee

Shrimp Harpin—Assorted Relish Tray—Freshly Baked Hot Breads—Mixed Fruits in Lemon Gelatin—Coffee

DINNER PARTIES

A sit down dinner party is always something extra special. In planning such an affair, keep in mind the number of people that can be seated comfortably at your table—usually no more than six or eight. The menu should be one that can be served without your leaving the table more than once. The first course may be a fruit or vegetable juice served by the host in the living room while you slip into the kitchen to attend to the food.

MENU SUGGESTIONS: Roast Beef—Noodle Pudding—Buttered Asparagus—Lettuce Wedges with French Dressing—Hot Rolls—Chocolate Cake—Coffee

Chicken with Peach Sauce—Browned Potatoes—Peas and Carrots—Tossed Salad—Hot Rolls— Vanilla Ice Cream Balls rolled in chopped pecans topped with Caramel Sauce—Coffee

Baked Ham—Candied Sweet Potatoes—Broccoli with Hollandaise Sauce—Molded Vegetable Salad—Hot Rolls—Coconut Cream Pie—Coffee

A MORNING COFFEE

A morning coffee is a relatively new form of entertaining. It may be used as a means of introducing a new comer on your street to her neighbors, for a committee meeting or the opportuniuty for a group to meet and talk informally with a candidate running for a local school or government office.

A tray of assorted sweet rolls, donuts and coffee cake with plenty of good coffee, takes care of refreshments.

DESSERT AND COFFEE

Dessert and coffee is the answer to the entertaining problem for those with limited time and a limited budget. You simply ask a few friends to drop in at 7:30 or 8 o'clock to have dessert or coffee with you. An evening of cards or watching favorite TV shows may follow. You may serve anywhere—at your dining table, a card table on the patio or at the coffee table in your living room. Since you have only one food to prepare, it can be a little more elaborate than the dessert you might serve with a regular dinner. For ideas on what to serve you might look at Dessert Suggestions in the chapter on baking.

MENU SUGGESTIONS: Angel Food Cake slices topped with Whipped Cream, Sweetened Fresh Strawberries or Sliced Peaches.
Apple or Blueberry Cobbler with Lemon Sauce
Cream Puff Shells filled with Vanilla Ice Cream, topped with Chocolate Sauce
Spice Cake topped with Nutmeg Sauce
Fruit Curry with Sugar Cookies
Fresh Coconut Cake
Chocolate or Lemon Chiffon Pie
Warm Apple Pie with Hard Sauce or Vanilla Ice Cream
Vanilla Ice Cream Ball rolled in pecans topped with Caramel Sauce.

AFTERNOON TEAS

Afternoon teas offer no nicer, easier or less expensive way to entertain for a special guest or to say "thank you" to a group you have had working with you on a civic, church or school project.

It is usually served from your dining table set with your prettiest accessories. Tea is served at one end of the table and coffee or punch at the other end. If the group is quite large, it is wise to ask two of your friends to pour. This leaves you free to greet guests as they arrive and replenish the refreshments as necessary.

MENU SUGGESTIONS: Little Open Sandwiches—Petits Fours—Nuts—Mints—Tea—Coffee
Dainty Tea Sandwiches—Sliced Fruit Cake—Bonbons—Nuts—Tea—Coffee
Tiny Biscuits filled with Deviled Ham—Small Cake Squares—Nuts—Mints—Coffee—Tea

COFFEE SECRETS

1. Measure coffee accurately.
2. Use freshly drawn water.
3. Serve coffee as soon as possible after brewing.
4. For best results always brew coffee at full capacity of coffee maker.
5. Never boil coffee.
6. Never reuse coffee grounds.
7. Keep coffee maker immaculately clean.
8. Always scald coffee maker before using.

DRIP COFFEE

Freshly ground coffee
Freshly boiled water

1. Pour water into kettle; cover; place over high heat until water boils.
2. Place filter in coffee basket; add coffee. Attach coffee basket to water container.
3. Pour boiling water into water container up to desired cup marking.
4. When dripping is completed, remove upper section immediately.
5. Stir brew; serve.
6. Maximum capacity 6 cups.

ICED COFFEE

16 tablespoons coffee
3 cups boiling water

1. Make coffee according to directions for drip coffee or percolator coffee.
2. Pour while hot into tall glasses filled with ice cubes.
3. Serve with sugar, cream.
4. Eight servings.

PERCOLATOR COFFEE

Freshly ground coffee
Freshly drawn hot water

1. Pour hot water into coffee pot up to desired cup marking.
2. Place coffee basket on stem; add coffee up to desired cup marking; adjust spreader.
3. Place stem and basket in coffee pot; cover.
4. Place over high heat; after perking starts, reduce heat to medium; perk 7-10 minutes.
5. Remove stem and basket immediately.
6. Maximum capacity 8 cups.

TEA

1. Use water that is fresh and boiling vigorously.
2. Warm teapot by rinsing with hot water.
3. Put a level teaspoon of tea or one tea bag into the teapot for every cup.
4. Pour boiling water on tea; cover.
5. Let tea brew five minutes; stir; serve.

CRANBERRY FRUIT PUNCH

6 pints cranberry juice cocktail
1½ quarts orange juice
2½ cups lemon juice
3 cups pineapple juice
3 cups sugar
1½ cups water

1. Combine all fruit juices.
2. Add sugar, water; mix thoroughly, until sugar dissolves.
3. Chill well or serve with ice cubes.
4. Fifty ½ cup servings.

Appetizer and Salad Suggestions

Celery stuffed with mixture of Roquefort and cream cheese—chopped liver with cracker or party rye—liver, mushrooms, pineapple broiled on small skewers—tiny cream puffs stuffed with hot crab or lobster meat—tiny pizzas made on 1-inch biscuit halves—canned sweet green peppers stuffed with tuna fish.

Canned fruit cocktail molded in cherry, raspberry or strawberry gelatin—grapefruit sections with sliced avocado and pineapple with French dressing—diced apple and celery with chopped nuts blended with mayonnaise—sliced cucumber and onions in sour cream blended with a little vinegar and sugar—cantaloupe and honeydew balls with French dressing—cole slaw with pieces of pineapple or shredded carrots.

HOW TO PLAN MENUS

When it comes to planning meals, most homemakers manage breakfast and lunch without too much difficulty. Dinner is quite often a different story especially when meal preparation is a new experience.

Usually, it is the important meal of the day—the one time when the family is together. It should be a well balanced meal, eaten leisurely and spiced with pleasant conversation. Because budgets, time, and personal likes and dislikes in foods must be taken into consideration, you can rarely use stock menus other than as a guide, so planning what to have for dinner is strictly up to you. Here's how.

Plan meals for three or four days at one time. This will enable you to have better meals with greater variety. It will also save shopping time and money and provide a good opportunity to use up leftovers.

Since meat is usually the most expensive item in your budget, this is the best place to start. Decide on the meat, fish or fowl, then plan the rest of the meal—one white, one green or yellow vegetable, salad and dessert—around it.

Variety is essential. Therefore, do not repeat the same kind or type of food in the same meal. If you have fruit in an appetizer or a salad, then don't repeat it in the dessert.

Contrast tart with sweet, bland and highly seasoned, fluid and solid, soft and crisp, hot and cold. Never have more than one strong flavored food in a meal. Two foods prepared the same way such as creamed chicken and creamed potatoes is also taboo. A browned potato or French fries would be better.

Good color combinations are of equal importance. Serve green or yellow vegetables with plain potatoes. Garnish white vegetables with chopped parsley, pimento or paprika. Do not serve all hot or all cold foods at the same meal. Even in summer, one hot dish is desirable while ices and crispy cold salads add interest to cold weather meals.

Many casserole dishes need only a tossed salad with a tart dressing and a good dessert to make an appetizing meal. Rice, macaroni, noodles, lima beans and corn are good substitutes for potatoes.

Try at least one or two new recipes each week. This will eliminate the sameness that can and often does creep into meals. Take advantage of the many convenience foods now on the market. Cake and pie crust mixes, frostings and canned pie fillings; tender, fluffy rolls and biscuits that need only be popped into the oven; frozen entrées that can be reheated while you prepare the rest of the dinner. Most of these convenience foods are of excellent quality, worthy of your consideration especially on days when food preparation time is limited.

With well planned menus, you will eat better for less money. Your meals will have greater variety and before you know it, the man in your life will be saying, "Honey, you are the best cook ever!"

DIETS AND DIETS

Overweight is almost always the direct result of consuming more food than the body requires. No two people will utilize the same amount of food even though the quantity they eat may be identical. That is why a special diet will give results to one person and not to another.

Today there are probably hundreds of crash diets in existence. A few are good, many are lacking in the vital elements essential to good health and some border on the ridiculous. We've gone through the egg diet, the banana diet, the rice diet, the calories don't count diet and the worst one of all, the vitamin pill and black coffee diet. Every few weeks a new one appears and people go on it without realizing that while their friend Bill lost five pounds in a week on that diet, they may not lose more than a pound.

If you are really serious about losing excess poundage, there is only one safe and sensible way to do it. Consult your physician. He will check your metabolism—the rate at which your body utilizes food—your general physical condition and prescribe a diet that is right for you. He may put you on a low calorie diet or he may tell you to eat your regular meals but eat smaller portions. This is an excellent rule to follow because foods prepared the New Method Way retain the valuable nutrients you may need and you can eat less without suffering hunger pains. Your doctor also may tell you to eat a good breakfast and to eliminate rich sauces and substitute fruit for rich desserts. If you conscientiously follow his advice, pounds will disappear gradually. You will feel better. You will look better.

GUIDE TO GOOD EATING

Milk: Use daily 3 or more glasses of milk for children—2 or more for adults. Cheese, ice cream and other milk made foods can supply part of the milk.

Meat: 2 or more servings meat, fish, poultry, eggs or cheese with dry beans, peas and nuts as alternates.

Vegetables and Fruits: 4 or more servings-including dark green or yellow vegetables, citrus fruits or tomatoes.

Breads and Cereals: 4 or more servings of enriched or whole grain breads and cereals of all kinds.

This is the foundation for a good diet. Use more of these or other foods as needed for growth, for activity and for desirable weight control.

These nutritional statements have been reviewed by the Council on Foods and Nutrition of the American Medical Association and found consistent with current authoritative opinion.

World's Most Modern Cooking Utensils

Wear-Ever's sleek, modern design captures the homemaker's dream of the perfect
cooking utensil with color-coordinated good looks that will last—carefree stainless steel
interiors so easy to clean. . . . extra-thick aluminum on the outside to help insure

For the Modern Home
Of Today
And Tomorrow

PLUS STAINLESS
WEAR EVER
ALUMINUM
INNER·CLAD ®

Method EQUIPMENT

COOKING ALL YOUR FOODS PERFECTLY

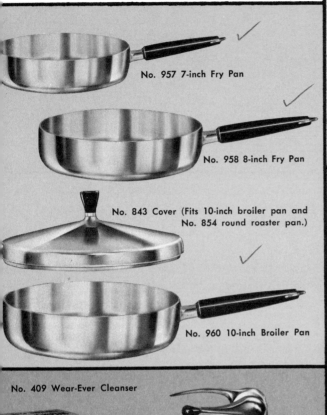

No. 957 7-inch Fry Pan

No. 958 8-inch Fry Pan

No. 843 Cover (Fits 10-inch broiler pan and No. 854 round roaster pan.)

No. 960 10-inch Broiler Pan

No. 409 Wear-Ever Cleanser

No. 258 Can Opener

No. 402 Holder

No. 968 Coffee Maker Combination*

No. 406 Filters (700)

No. 818 Cover*

No. 918 Utility Pan*

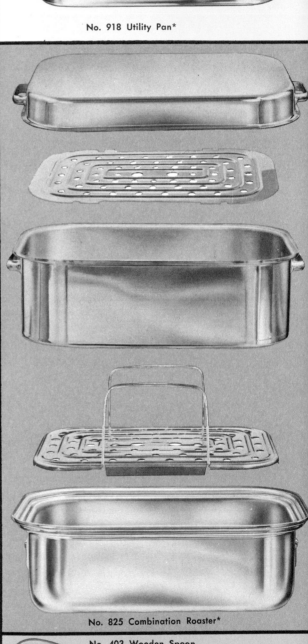

No. 825 Combination Roaster*

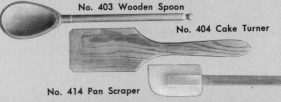

No. 403 Wooden Spoon

No. 404 Cake Turner

No. 414 Pan Scraper

HOW TO CARE
FOR
WEAR-EVER
NEW
METHOD UTENSILS

DAILY CARE: After food has been lifted, fill pan with warm water then wash, rinse, and dry. Utensils should not be allowed to soak in dishwater as it could mar the finish.

ELECTRIC DISHWASHERS: Since some local waters combined with detergents can mar the exterior finish, washing utensils in an electric dishwasher is not recommended.

TO REMOVE BURNED FOOD: If food should accidentally burn onto inside of utensil, partially fill pan with water, boil a few minutes, then scrape off burned food with a wooden spoon.

TO POLISH OUTSIDE: To polish outside of utensil use any good silver polish or a little Bon Ami with a steel wool and soap pad that is very wet and soft.

TO POLISH INSIDE: To restore the original luster to the inside of the utensil, use the following cleaning procedures:

Stainless lined utensil—The mottled, iridescent or yellow staining commonly called "heat tint" which may develop on the interior stainless steel surface can be removed with any good stainless steel cleaner available at food markets. These stain removers should be used on the stainless steel inner surface only. Any accidental spillage on the aluminium exterior should be rinsed off immediately.

All-aluminum utensil—Rub briskly with a wet steel wool and soap pad; rinse; dry. Remove any harmless discoloration caused by minerals present in foods and some waters by boiling a solution of two tablespoons cream of tartar per quart of water in the pan 10–15 minutes.

ALUMILITE COVERS: The Alumilite finish on covers can be kept clean and beautiful by washing in hot sudsy water. Do not use steel wool or other abrasives on this finish. Do not wash covers in an electric dishwasher.

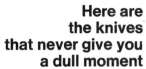
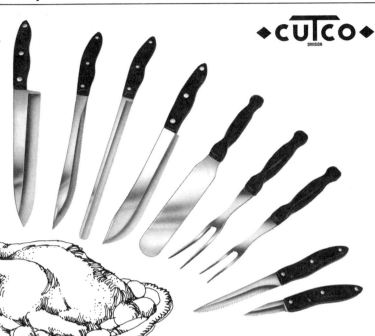
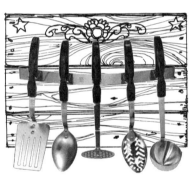

If You Need Service

Your Wear-Ever New Method Equipment is designed and manufactured to give you many years of satisfaction. Complete information on best ways to care and clean your Wear-Ever is contained on page 96. But, if you feel you are in need of additional information or if you need service, contact your Wear-Ever New Method Distributor or write to:

**SERVICE
WEAR-EVER NEW METHOD UTENSILS
1089 EASTERN AVENUE
CHILLICOTHE, OHIO 45601**

GIVE DETAILS OF SERVICE NEEDED INCLUDING THE NUMBERS ON THE BOTTOM SIDE OF EACH PAN TO BE SERVICED.

The Wear-Ever Trademark has stood for Quality, Service and Fair Dealing for over 65 years.

WEAR·EVER SUBSIDIARY OF ALCOA